The Philadelphia Inquirer

Philly's Final Four

UConn Rocks the Cradle of Women's Basketball

By the staff of The Philadelphia Inquirer

On the Cover: The Connecticut Huskies whooped it up after routing Tennessee, 71-52, for the NCAA women's basketball title at Philadelphia's sold-out First Union Center. Clockwise from the top: Tamika Williams, Swin Cash, Shea Ralph, Svetlana Abrosimova, Sue Bird (back to camera) and Asjha Jones. (Photo by Vicki Valerio)

On the Back Cover: Connecticut's Shea Ralph (left) scrapped with Tennessee's Kara Lawson for a loose ball in the national championship game. (Photo by Ron Cortes)

ISBN 1-58822-000-1

Table of Contents

Foreword

Women's college basketball needed Philadelphia. The breeding ground for the game, with its rich history and widespread progeny, the City of Brotherly Love was the ideal locale to hold the preeminent event in the women's game, the Final Four.

Philadelphians remembered tiny Immaculata College and its three national titles won in an era — the '70s — when disco dancers, not female athletes, were queen. They embraced the scores of coaches who, as children, played the game on blacktop courts scattered throughout the city. And, most important, they cared about the game.

As intensely as Philadelphians crave cheesesteaks and soft pretzels, they cared about Rene Portland, a Broomall native and the longtime Penn State coach who, alongside Theresa Grentz, led Cathy Rush's Mighty Macs to that trio of titles, but as a coach had never been to a Final Four. They cared about the slick, wavy-haired Geno Auriemma of Norristown, as outspoken a coach — men's or women's — as there is, and with one national title to his credit at Connecticut, one of the best. Like Temple coach John Chaney, they adored the driven Vivian Stringer, a recent arrival at Rutgers after leading two other programs to the Final Four. And they loved so many others: Notre Dame's Muffet McGraw, Vanderbilt's Jim Foster, and, of course, St. Joseph's coach Stephanie Gaitley.

So the announcement that, yes, Philadelphia would

become the first Northeastern city to host the Final Four in 2000 was embraced with great excitement, pride and vigor. If the city was hospitable enough to host a merry-making mixture of Republicans for their national convention, it could impress more than 300 Division I coaches, four teams, and a gaggle of supporters and fans of the game.

At the time, a title game matching the two best teams and two powerhouse programs in college hoops was merely an aspiration. And the organizing committee, astutely named Philadelphia Women's Basketball 2000 and under the leadership of a spark-plug New Yorker named Cathy Andruzzi, had more pressing issues, such as fund-raising.

With inexhaustible energy and enthusiasm, Andruzzi attacked the challenge of selling the Final Four to corporate Philadelphia. Because of NCAA restrictions, she couldn't offer sponsors signage inside the First Union Center, but she did have a coveted commodity: tickets to the event, which sold out in record time — a matter of hours.

With PWB 2000 omnipresent in the corporate community, the 1999-2000 season got under way with Auriemma's Connecticut Huskies atop the national polls. Pat Summitt's Tennessee Volunteers were looming in the shadows, as were Rutgers, Notre Dame, Louisiana Tech and Georgia. Everyone was shooting for Philadelphia.

"Playing in Philly would be a blast. An absolute blast," McGraw, a West Chester native and St. Joe's alumnus, said in October, encapsulating the feeling of all women's coaches, regardless of their Philadelphia connections. "It would be awesome. Absolutely awesome."

What was awesome was the buzz in Philly. In December, Tennessee came to town to take on St. Joe's. It was a homecoming for Vols guard Kristen "Ace" Clement, a legend from Cardinal O'Hara High School and a key component in Tennessee's quest to send Pat Summitt to her 12th Final Four.

After they blitzed St. Joe's, the Vols joined the Hawks for an autograph session. The next month, Connecticut, still toting the No. 1 ranking, visited the Philadelphia area. After beating Villanova, the Huskies took in a 76ers game at the First Union Center. As the season wore on, Notre Dame, Rutgers and Penn State all popped in for visits.

But perhaps the most intriguing games of the regular season occurred in venues outside the state. For the first time in women's basketball, Tennessee and Connecticut scheduled a home-and-home series, with the first game in Knoxville, Tenn., in January, followed by a February meeting in Storrs, Conn.

It was a made-for-ESPN event that took some coaxing of Auriemma and Summitt, both of whom were leery of the repercussions of going 0-2 in the series. That didn't happen, and after Tennessee won at Gampel Pavilion to even the series, observers were pointing toward Philly and a rubber match.

After Connecticut won the Big East tournament and Tennessee prevailed, again, in the Southeastern Conference tourney, the stage was set. Both teams drew No. 1 seeds in the tournament, along with Louisiana Tech, which would say goodbye to legendary coach Leon Barmore, who announced his retirement before the NCAA tournament began. He later changed his mind. Georgia, which earlier in the season dealt the Vols their worst SEC loss ever, was the top seed in the West.

As the tournament began on 16 college campuses across the country, PWB 2000 received grants from the city and state to complete its fund-raising efforts. After celebrity lunches, corporate contributions and a few tense moments — three months out, PWB 2000 was more than $500,000 shy of its goal — Andruzzi and her team had won. All that was left was to crown a champion.

The Final Four was exquisite. A record number of reporters told the stories of Tennessee and Rutgers, Connecticut and Penn State. Not only did three of the four coaches have Philly ties, so did key players, such as the Nittany Lions' Andrea Garner, the Scarlet Knights' Shawnetta Stewart and the Vols' Clement.

The Philadelphia Inquirer was there through it all — PWB 2000's struggles and triumphs, the entertaining regular season, the early rounds of the tournament and, finally, the climactic finale between No. 1 and No. 2, Connecticut and Tennessee. College basketball got what it wanted, a marquee matchup forecast in the preseason. And Auriemma's Huskies got what they wanted, unequivocal bragging rights and a second national championship trophy.

— Ashley McGeachy

Chapter 1

The Cradle of Basketball

The Quiet Revolution: Where It All Began

The birth of modern women's basketball was a noisy one. In the early 1970s, on Immaculata College's leafy Chester County campus, the groundbreaking success of that tiny Catholic school's team took place amid the racket of spoons drumming on metal buckets, the crackle of a walkie-talkie that kept coach Cathy Rush in touch with her husband, and the clatter of wheelchairs in the normally silent hallways of Camilla Hall.

"Camilla Hall is a place on Immaculata's campus where old and sick nuns are cared for," Rush recalls. "These nuns became so taken with our success that they used to pipe in the radio broadcasts of our games on the loudspeaker system. If we were losing at halftime, someone would come on the system and announce, 'Sisters, the

Immaculata coach Cathy Rush (shown in 1975) introduced men's techniques to her players.

Mighty Macs are in trouble!'

"And just like that, you'd have all these old nuns in wheelchairs or with canes and walkers coming down the hallways toward the chapel, gathering there for prayers to help us win."

The younger Immaculate Heart of Mary nuns attended games in person. And since player Rene Muth's father, Louis, owned a hardware store, they were provided with buckets and washboards that they smacked and scraped in heavenly delight as the Mighty Macs won the first three women's national championships between 1972 and 1974.

"You look back on that little school, with all these non-scholarship players from the Catholic League, and you wonder how we did it," says Denise Conway Crawford, who played on those teams. "I was one of five girls from Archbishop Prendergast [in Upper Darby] and I was the only one who had played in high school.

"The only answer I have," she says, "is that it was providential."

If, in another way, the Mighty Macs' success can be attributed to a man upstairs, that man would be Rush's husband, Ed. A National Basketball Association referee, he would find a lofty seat at each Immaculata game and, via walkie-talkie, relay advice to his wife on the bench. His NBA connections also helped introduce Cathy Rush to leading men's coaches, and she, unlike many of her counterparts at the time, was not shy about incorporating their methods.

Today, nearly three decades after Rush's tunic-clad teams helped create the cultural phenomenon, big-time women's sports is a television staple. Women's basketball, particularly at the professional level, fills big arenas in big cities. Not many people remember that Immaculata was in

Photo courtesy of Immaculata College

The 1972 Mighty Macs championship team. Bottom row (from left): Maureen Stuhlman, Rene Muth, Patricia Opilia, Maureen Mooney, Theresa Shank and Denise Conway. Top row: Coach Cathy Rush, Janet Young, Sue O'Grady, Janet Ruch, Judy Marra and student manager Rene Mack. Inset: Betty Ann Hoffman.

at the start, playing the first women's contests at Madison Square Garden and Philadelphia's Spectrum.

More significantly, Immaculata's success inspired an army of coaches, many of them Rush disciples. Her summer camps became a mecca for anyone interested in learning the game. In 1972, when Title IX suddenly required colleges to spend equitably on men's and women's sports, schools raced to Rush's camps to fill their basketball programs with coaches and players schooled in her technique.

Soon a "cheesesteak chain" of Philadelphia coaches such as Vivian Stringer, now at Rutgers, Jim Foster of Vanderbilt, Connecticut's Geno Auriemma and three of

Rush's Immaculata stars — Theresa Shank Grentz, Marianne Crawford Stanley and Rene Muth Portland — stretched across the country. The coaches formed a network of evangelists for a sleek and compelling sport, one that only a few years before had been played with byzantine rules in cramped gymnasiums by women in skirts. Modern women's basketball took root in places such as Storrs, Conn., Chattanooga, Tenn., and Los Angeles. Now there are universities where women's games outdraw the men's. College teams have multimillion-dollar budgets and play in huge arenas. Women's coaches get perks once reserved for football coaches, and college stars can even keep playing after graduation in the WNBA.

On March 31 and April 2, with hoopla and media coverage unimaginable in 1972 when Immaculata won the first national tournament in Normal, Ill., the women's Final Four was contested back in the cradle, Philadelphia. The hallways at the arena, the glittering First Union Center, were packed with exhibits about the game's history. The chronology focused heavily on Philadelphia and the legend of the Mighty Macs.

"It was like Camelot," says Grentz, the 1992 Olympic coach who now is at Illinois. "I often go back to Immaculata to be around all those memories. It was wonderful."

Ironically, Immaculata itself has gone quiet. After being catapulted to prominence, its program eventually was shoved into the Division III shadows. When Rush left at the end of the 1977 season, she predicted that the demands of Title IX and the heftier budgets of much larger schools would doom Immaculata. She was right.

Now it is the big state schools, the Connecticuts, Tennessees and North Carolinas, that dominate with their state-of-the-art facilities and scholarship-laden teams. Wayland Baptist, Delta State and Immaculata, the small colleges that populated the game's quaint early years, have become nothing but curious historical footnotes.

"You see all these big schools spending all this money on their women's teams and it's hard to believe," Crawford says. "Our gym burned down in 1967 and we had to practice in the motherhouse across the street. When we went to the first tournament, we had to sell toothbrushes to raise enough money. And even then, only one coach and eight of the 11 girls could go. We flew standby, stayed four in a room and washed our own uniforms in the sink after every game."

Why Philadelphia? The Catholic League, with its feeder system of parochial school teams, helped considerably. It provided top-notch coaching and excellent quality of play. An entire generation of early stars such as June Olkowski and twins Mary and Patty Coyle played in the league.

Very quickly this small universe produced all sorts of intertwined connections. Theresa Shank, for example, married Karl Grentz Jr., whose mother had coached Shank's Immaculata teammate Judy Marra Martelli at St. Dorothy's in Drexel Hill. Martelli met her husband, St. Joseph's men's coach Phil Martelli, at Rush's summer camp. Through that camp, Phil Martelli got his friend, Geno Auriemma, who worked with Jim Foster at Bishop McDevitt, an assistant's job at the University of Virginia.

They were like dandelions, popping up everywhere, all somehow linked to a single flower that bloomed briefly on the Immaculata campus near Frazer. Soon the game caught on in the Public League. In 1981, Dobbins' Linda Page became the first high school player to score 100 points in a game. Within a decade, Dawn Staley became one of the sport's great point guards.

"You can't go anywhere without running into coaches with a Philadelphia connection," said Auriemma, a former Norristown resident who has won two national championships and built a powerhouse program at Connecticut. "It's amazing. It's such a small world."

None of the players on Immaculata's championship teams came to the school of 550 students specifically for basketball. But most shared a common background. Portland and Martelli had played at nearby Villa Maria Academy, and the rest of the Mighty Macs had attended Catholic League schools.

"These girls came to college having experienced the Catholic League, the crowds, the pressure, all that," Rush says. "It was a big advantage."

In fact, Rush often scheduled scrimmages against Catholic League teams, knowing she'd find better competition there than at other local colleges.

If Immaculata is the messiah in the story of women's basketball, then West Chester University, just a few miles to the southwest, is John the Baptist, preparing the way.

Try to remember what women's basketball was like in the late 1960s. Although it was played at colleges and high schools, it barely rose above the level of a gym-class pastime. Girls in tunics played a rigidly controlled game in which even the number of dribbles was regulated. There were no independent leagues, no college scholarships and certainly no legitimate professional leagues.

But during those years, the Philadelphia area was home to a relatively strong tradition of women's collegiate sports — even though that competition generally took place in a vacuum, attracting little interest beyond the campus walls.

"Way before anyone else, this area was at the forefront of women's sports," says Mimi Greenwood. In 1969 she headed women's athletics at West Chester, though her title listed her as an "adviser" to the school's athletic director. "Since probably as far back as the 1940s, there were very successful field hockey, swimming and lacrosse programs around here. There was a kind of English tradition at work in the local schools, a feeling that athletics ought to be a part of a genteel woman's education."

That attitude, Greenwood says, can be traced to Constance Appleby, an English-born professor at Bryn Mawr College who introduced field hockey to the United States early in the 20th century.

"She was definitely at the forefront of women's sports," Greenwood says. "She believed that athletics contributed to the well-rounded woman, just as it did the well-rounded man." Appleby died in 1981 at the age of 107.

Despite that liberal attitude, basketball was considered too rough-and-tumble for genteel women, and by the late 1960s it was still a very minor sport at most local colleges.

"When I was first asked to start a [women's basketball rankings] poll in the mid-'70s, I resisted," says Inquirer sportswriter Mel Greenberg. "The philosophy of the AIAW [the Association for Intercollegiate Athletics for Women, the first overarching national regulatory body for the sport] was that if we started getting newspaper stories about women's basketball, it would open them up to all the evils of the men's game."

Still, if women's basketball ever was going to take off, Philadelphia figured to be the place it would happen.

"It's not surprising that the women's game kind of took root here, because there was a pretty unique tradition in

VICKI VALERIO / Inquirer Staff Photographer

Unlike the '70s, girls learn the game these days when they are very young. Above, Vidalina Rodriguez fired up a foul shot in the 10-and-under league run by the Philadelphia Recreation Department. At right, teammates Shamyra Hammond (left) and Tenea Wilson discussed strategy with Rodriguez.

Philadelphia," says Greenwood, now retired and living in Aldan, Pa. "The high schools, particularly in Delaware County, had some strong teams and rivalries. So did colleges like Penn, Temple, Ursinus and West Chester.

"And there were a number of basketball leagues for older women, usually affiliated with their workplaces," she says. "There were nursing leagues and teachers' leagues and one known as the warehouse league because its players worked at the old American Stores warehouses."

West Chester, because its education-based curriculum traditionally attracted women and because it had a strong physical education department, was particularly strong in women's athletics. Lucille Kyvallos of West Chester coached a young woman named Cathy Rush in the mid-1960s. Later, Carol Eckman coached teams that were among the first to drop the six-player format in favor of men's rules.

At the time, the National Collegiate Athletic Association was strictly a men's club. There was no women's equivalent to the men's postseason NCAA tournament or even the National Invitation Tournament. Women's sports were regulated informally by an ad hoc committee of educators called the Division of Girls and Women's Sports (DGWS).

Kyvallos and later Eckman, with the blessing of West Chester athletic director Robert Reese, began to urge the DGWS to institute some sort of postseason basketball tournament for the better women's teams. They realized it wouldn't be an easy task.

Outside of the individual schools and their opponents, who knew anything about these teams? They got little fan support and even less media coverage. And since women's rules wouldn't become standardized until 1971, there was no objective way to judge a team's quality. Schools in different states played with widely varied guidelines. Some used men's rules, some a shot clock. Others played with three women stationed on each side of half-court. Still others employed a hybrid game in which five offensive players went against six defenders.

After years of lobbying, Eckman finally got permission to plan the event in 1969.

The 16 teams that competed in the National Invitational Collegiate Women's Basketball Tournament at West Chester that March were a curious amalgam — small and large schools, some with great men's basketball traditions, others with none. They were: West Chester, Western Carolina, Iowa Wesleyan, Iowa, Northeastern, Lynchburg, Southern Connecticut, Ohio State, Purdue, Kentucky, Dayton, Ursinus, Central Michigan, Ball State, Southern Illinois and Towson State.

In the final game, which according to newspaper accounts attracted about 2,000 fans to Hollinger Fieldhouse, West Chester defeated Western Carolina.

By 1972, Title IX was law, the tiny National Invitational was history and the AIAW hosted its first national tournament with a different collection of 16 teams, including Immaculata.

"We had no idea what a tournament like that was," Immaculata's Crawford says. "It just wasn't something any of us had any experience with. But Cathy was so competitive that we knew she'd get us ready."

Rush was hired by Immaculata one year before the tournament at a salary of $450 per year. Her 1971 team played 12 games against driving-distance opponents. It won 10.

Urged by her husband to challenge the women with

more competitive foes, Rush upgraded the schedule for the 1971-'72 season. The team went 24-1 and in the insular world of Immaculata's campus became a phenomenon. Rush was a pioneer. She incorporated physical picks and trapping defenses into her teaching, something other women's coaches were slow to accept.

"So many of the women's coaches then were older. They had been raised on the six-on-six games, so naturally they were less likely to incorporate anything new into their teaching," says Marra Martelli, a reserve on Rush's championship teams. "Cathy wasn't afraid to use that stuff. She wasn't afraid to step over the line. She'd have coaches like Jim Valvano [of North Carolina State] and Herbie Magee [of what was then Philadelphia Textile] come to her camps and she'd pick their brains."

Immaculata's only loss that season came, not surprisingly, to West Chester: a 70-38 drubbing in the final of the regional qualifying portion of the tournament.

Both were invited to the AIAW tourney in Normal, Ill., but Immaculata, seeded 15th out of 16 teams, wasn't sure it could make the trip. The team eventually sold enough toothbrushes to get a traveling party of nine to Normal.

In the final, the Mighty Macs met West Chester again.

"That was a team that might have beaten us nine out of 10 times," Crawford recalls. "But like I said, there was something providential at work. And we won [52-48]."

Rush's club would win the AIAW crown again in 1973 and '74, and then lose in two straight championship games to Delta State of Louisiana. But by then the Macs had pushed women's basketball into the periphery of big-time sports. In fact, the Mighty Macs' 1975 game against Maryland was the first women's contest to be nationally televised. They played Queens College at Madison Square

Garden and drew 11,969 fans. National publications chronicled the curious story of this tiny college with it noisy, prayerful fan base.

By 1977, when Immaculata was eliminated by LSU in the national semifinals, Rush saw the game's future taking shape. The NCAA would take over the tournament in 1982, ensuring that the big schools would be the best positioned to recruit and spend money. Something special — the innocence, the fun — would be sacrificed. So Rush quit and, despite numerous offers to return, has stayed away from coaching.

Now, wherever Rush or her players go, they are asked about the Mighty Macs by those who witnessed the phenomenon and those who wished they had.

"It was crazy," Rush says. "It was wonderful. It will never happen again."

Rush's Immaculata players, like Portland and Grentz, had to wash their uniforms and sell candy bars to pay for travel. A quarter century later, the Tennessee Volunteers, like several of the top teams, take charter flights to and from games and have a full support staff of trainers, managers and assistants to tend to their every need.

— *Frank Fitzpatrick*

Mel Greenberg, a Philadelphia Inquirer sportswriter, was a pioneer when it came to covering the women's game.

Long before newspapers began covering games, and years ahead of networks putting the women on TV, Greenberg was hard at work covering and promoting women's college basketball.

He created and ran the first Associated Press women's poll, collecting data from around the country

Dawn Staley got Mel Greenberg's autograph.

using a phone bank set up and manned by volunteers he recruited with the promise of free pizza.

Greenberg was forever championing the sport, regardless of how much money it earned or how many people went to games.

How He Became Mr. Women's Basketball

Mel Greenberg has been called Mr. Women's Basketball, which is an intriguing title but not terribly descriptive. What does it mean? Did he invent women's basketball? Marry someone important in the game? Coach the women's Dream Team?

The answer is none of the above.

Greenberg earned that moniker by being just about the first person — besides the players, coaches and their families — to care about women's basketball.

As a Philadelphia Inquirer sportswriter, he recognized the players' grit and savvy. He told anyone he could buttonhole — and Mel is one of the great buttonholers in history — that the women played the game right.

Mel Greenberg was (and is) equal parts journalist, fan and impresario. (OK, so shoot him. He does not regard his subject from an ironic distance, as journalists are trained to do.)

His lasting contribution was to help organize the universe of women's basketball by creating a ranking system that let everyone know who the top teams were — which ones were on the rise, and which were falling from their perch.

The men's rankings, voted on by coaches and sportswriters, have long been part of the narrative of a college season. But before Mel started his poll in 1976, no one had ever done the equivalent for the women's game.

We asked Mel to talk a little about the evolution of women's basketball and his place in it:

Q: Were you always partial to women's basketball?

A: You can't like what you can't see. It wasn't on TV or publicized much at all, so I didn't really have much exposure to it.

Q: So did you just stumble into the wrong gym one day and come upon this parallel world of fierce women draining jump shots and taking it to the hoop?

A: No, not exactly. One day in 1974 my friend Dick Weiss — who is known as Dickie Hoops and is probably the leading men's college basketball writer in the country — dragged me to this hidden-away gym inside Pearson Hall at Temple. Temple was playing Immaculata College. There couldn't have been more than 40 people in the stands. "You've got to see the way these girls play," Weiss boasted to me, referring to Immaculata.

Q: And how did they play?

A: For those of us who grew up watching men's basketball in the 1960s, it was basketball the way we remembered it. I had been manager of Temple's basketball team under the legendary coach Harry Litwack the year they won the National Invitation Tournament. The women played like Litwack's teams, with an emphasis on passing and teamwork, not individual play.

Q: You started the national women's basketball poll in 1976. How did that come about?

A: I had been covering women's games for The Inquirer when Jay Searcy, who was the sports editor, asked me to start a poll. I told him he was nuts. You have to understand, the game was really in the dark ages. Some of the coaches didn't even know the records of their next opponent.

Q: So you filled an information vacuum.

A: Exactly. I became the clearinghouse. To do the poll, I talked to 50 or 60 coaches a week. There weren't computers and e-mail in the beginning, so I had a lot of help. We put in long hours and ordered a lot of takeout pizza.

Q: Who's the best women's player you've ever seen?

A: It's not clear-cut, but right up at the top would be Cheryl Miller and Nancy Lieberman-Cline.

Q: But they're relative old-timers.

A: Yeah, but they could do so much with the basketball. Among the moderns, I would put Chamique Holdsclaw on the list, for her athleticism and moves around the hoop. But she's not as skilled yet as those two were.

VICKI VALERIO / Inquirer Staff Photographer

All for one, teammates from the Happy Hollow Rec Center joined hands before their 10-and-under league game.

Q: The women's game used to be a little secret and you were one of the few people in on it. It's much bigger now. Do you miss anything about the old days?

A: As a journalist, I like it better now. You don't hear the same stupid questions, like "Where did you learn to play?" That was a big one. Now, it's understood the women have places to play and role models. You just go out and cover the game. It's basketball.

Q: The Women's Basketball Coaches Association gave you its first annual media award in 1991, then named the award after you. Is that a source of pride?

A: To tell you the truth, I was already well-known in that world. The best thing about the award was that it caused The Inquirer to discover me. I had been like one of those NFL games televised nationally, but blacked out in my home market. Until I got the award, I don't think anyone back here realized the poll had become a big thing.

— *Michael Sokolove*

VICKI VALERIO / Inquirer Staff Photographer

Davalyn Cunningham (left) of Rutgers and Asjha Jones of
Connecticut fought for position during a Big East battle.
UConn beat the Scarlet Knights twice during the regular sea-
son and once in the final of the conference tournament.

Chapter 2

In Search of 64

Before the season began, Connecticut and Tennessee were ranked No. 1 and No. 2 in everyone's preseason polls. From the beginning, it seemed like a foregone conclusion that the two titans of the women's game would be coming to Philadelphia for the Final Four. The only unanswered question seemed to be which two teams would join them. No matter who made it for Final Four weekend, one thing seemed clear: This Final Four would have a distinctly Philly flavor.

From the Start, a Philly Feel to the Rankings

The top teams in the Associated Press preseason poll had several ties to Philadelphia. That seemed only fitting, since the season would end here at the Final Four.

Rutgers, ranked No. 4 in the preseason, is just 75 minutes from Philadelphia. The team was coached by Vivian Stringer, whose coaching career began at Cheyney State in

1970. Scarlet Knights guard Shawnetta Stewart, a University City graduate known as "Baby Barkley," was a key player on a squad loaded with talent.

The top team, Connecticut, with 29 first-place votes and 1,071 points in the sportswriters' poll, was coached by Geno Auriemma, who grew up in Norristown.

The No. 2 team, Tennessee, with eight first-place votes and 1,032 points, was counting on junior Kristen "Ace" Clement, a Cardinal O'Hara High graduate, to run coach Pat Summitt's offense.

Two other teams in the top 10 also had local ties. No. 8 Notre Dame was coached by former St. Joseph's star Muffet McGraw, while No. 10 Penn State was coached by former Immaculata star Rene Portland. The Nittany Lions featured senior Andrea Garner of Masterman High and sophomore Rashana Barnes, a West Catholic High graduate.

No. 12 Illinois was coached by yet another former Immaculata star, Theresa Grentz. And the coach of No. 18 Kansas was Marian Washington, who played on West Chester's championship team in 1969.

St. Joseph's received honorable mention in the preseason poll. Coach Stephanie Gaitley hoped the Hawks' rugged schedule could propel her squad into the upper tier of the 315 women's teams in Division I.

Connecticut's top ranking marked the first time that a school had both its men's and women's teams begin at No. 1 in the AP poll. The Huskies men's team was the defending national champion.

— *Mel Greenberg*

ERIC MENCHER / Inquirer Staff Photographer

St. Joseph's Kathy Costello hit the floor in a fight for a loose ball with Tennessee's Semeka Randall. The Volunteers flexed their muscles in an 82-59 victory.

Tennessee Comes to Town

Philadelphia got its first taste of big-time basketball on Dec. 19 when Tennessee, toting the No. 2 national ranking, visited St. Joseph's Alumni Memorial Fieldhouse. It was a planned homecoming for Volunteers junior guard Kristen "Ace" Clement, an all-American from Cardinal O'Hara High. Clement, then the starting point guard, had more than 100 family members, friends and fans in the stands, and coach Pat Summitt wanted her to have a dress

VICKI VALERIO / Inquirer Staff Photographer

After the Vols wrapped up the Southeastern Conference championship, Kristen Clement snipped a piece of the net. Tennessee won the SEC tournament with a 70-67 win over Mississippi State.

rehearsal at home in case the Vols reached the Final Four.

It took only a few minutes on Hawk Hill for Tennessee to take control. The Volunteers quickly stifled St. Joseph's with an 8-0 opening run and went unchallenged the rest of the way for an 82-59 victory.

A standing-room-only crowd of more than 3,200 included former Vols star Chamique Holdsclaw and a large group of former Hawks players.

"I'm really proud of our team tonight," Summitt said afterward. "I thought they came in here really focused and took an impressive St. Joseph's team out early. I thought we played with a lot of poise."

Clement, a prized recruit when Tennessee visited St. Joe's three seasons earlier, scored 10 points. "With Ace coming home, it was important for her to maintain her focus," Summitt said of Clement's performance, which featured one flashy no-look pass to teammate Semeka Randall for an easy basket. "I have to compliment her. She set the pace for us, kept her focus, and she did what had to be done."

Summitt also wanted the rest of her players to enjoy a taste of Philadelphia, even though Alumni Memorial Fieldhouse paled in size to the First Union Center. "We want to be back here," Summitt said. "We know we have some improving to do, but I think we're on the right path right now."

Tennessee enjoyed a 37-28 rebounding advantage in the game. Also, the Hawks had 24 turnovers. The outcome was somewhat disappointing to St. Joseph's, which looked eagerly to the matchup, especially after an earlier win over Stanford.

"I don't want to take anything away from Tennessee," Hawks coach Stephanie Gaitley said. "They are an elite program. We took a gamble with our schedule. There's a gap between the top, premier programs and us. These games allow us the opportunity to learn how to close the gap."

— *Mel Greenberg*

After the game, the gym was crowded for an autograph session, which was planned for the St. Joe's players. But with Clement leading the way, the Vols also participated. Inquirer columnist Claire Smith was there.

Volunteers Are as Good as Advertised

The big girls St. Joseph's wanted the most finally arrived in Philadelphia in the form of the mighty Tennessee Volunteers. What unfolded was a graphic reminder that there may be no greater distance in sports than the five best teams in women's college sports and those merely aspiring to visit the top 25.

The Volunteers, the nation's second-ranked team, proved that there are 7-1 teams and then there are 7-1 juggernauts, as they dismantled the Hawks in much the way they have most all comers this year.

Tennessee awed a standing-room-only crowd at St. Joe's Fieldhouse and brought the high-soaring Hawks closer to earth and reality. Most important, the Volunteers inspired not so much the adults in the house who came to see what all the fuss about the women's team of the '90s was about. The more important impact was on the girls. Hundreds and hundreds of girls were treated to another segment of a year-long coming-out party that started with the women's World Cup soccer team intrigue and ended with a national college basketball champion being crowned in their own backyards.

If the squeals that prepubescent girls usually reserve for rock stars and Derek Jeter were any indication, the up-and-coming generations dream not only about 'N Sync, the Backstreet Boys and "The Rock," but about being the next Kristen "Ace" Clement, Tamika Catchings and Semeka Randall.

The welcome and the interest underscored the city's willingness to extend the game to both genders. No one felt the embrace more than Clement, the former Broomall resident whose hometown contingent consisted of more than

150.

"It felt great coming back to the community, seeing a lot of friends from high school, a lot of young players who looked up to me in high school," the savvy junior guard said.

It never hurts when the grown-up versions of the next generation's sports heroes actually live up to their billing. Tennessee, a program that seeks play in future tournament sites, did just that, from the moment the Vols arrived, attracting crowds around their arriving bus that rivaled an Allen Iverson entourage. And once Pat Summitt's interchangeable all-Americans donned their signature orange togs, Hawk Hill was transformed into Rocky Top and the clinic was on.

— *Claire Smith*

The day after the game, Summitt helped Philadelphia Women's Basketball 2000 with its fund-raising efforts. She was the keynote speaker at a $75-a-plate luncheon at Park Hyatt at the Bellevue, an event that raised $30,000, and she told the crowd: "I hope I'm working" on Final Four weekend.

Pat Summitt Volunteers Her Time

Pat Summitt knows about women's basketball. She has been coaching for 26 years — "I was in over my head," she said of her early years — and by mid-December her Tennessee teams had been ranked 379 times in the 24-year history of the weekly Associated Press women's poll, missing just 14 times.

Noting that she was just a junior in high school when the first women's national championship was played at

VICKI VALERIO / Inquirer Staff Photographer

Coach Pat Summitt directed her team during Tennessee's triumph over Mississippi State in the Southeastern Conference title game.

West Chester State College in 1969, Summitt said that fund-raising, once nonexistent for women's sports, had helped the tournament grow.

"Corporate America, we love you," Summitt said.

Cathy Andruzzi, the executive director of the organizing committee, said that $1.4 million was needed to host the event.

"We're halfway there," said Andruzzi.

Among the crowd of 450 that included representatives from many local colleges was former Immaculata coach Cathy Rush. Earlier in the season, she was elected to the second class of the new Women's Basketball Hall of Fame in Knoxville, Tenn. Summitt was inducted in June 1999 when the facility opened.

"I see all this, and I am just flabbergasted," Rush said of the media and financial blitz associated with the tournament.

Summitt said the fact that Philadelphia in 1995 aggressively pursued the finals "speaks volumes."

"Now, we're seeing active bidding for this event all over the country," she said.

Former Mayor Edward G. Rendell and new Mayor John Street were among the opening greeters who urged financial support from the corporate community. Street promised "the full cooperation of the new administration" in hosting the tournament. Rendell, noting that it would be held for the first time in a Northeastern city, called for the finals to be the "best ever."

Rendell alluded to the city's hosting of the presidential summit and the summer's Republican National Convention. "We never fail to do a first-class job," Rendell said. "We do them right, and we do them well."

But with a little more than three months to go before

the Final Four, the organizing committee was still more than a half-million dollars shy of its fund-raising goal. Would Hoop City have to be scaled back? Would events or transportation have to be cut? Certainly someone had extra cash left after the holidays.

— *Mel Greenberg*

While planning forged ahead for staging the Final Four and the regular season progressed, the organizing committee in Philadelphia was finding fund-raising to be a difficult chore. As the calendar changed to a new year, Philadelphia Women's Basketball 2000 was still beating down the doors of corporate board rooms, looking for money.

The Organizers' Mad Dash for Cash

For those who had a quarter million left over after holiday buying sprees, here's what the women's Final Four at the First Union Center was offering:

Fifty tickets to the semifinals and the final; sixteen parking passes to the team practice sessions and 20 parking passes to the games; 30 invitations to the pregame party and 30 more to the VIP/media party; eight exclusive, commemorative, limited-edition gifts.

There were other perks, of course, but no one could fault you if you were still unwilling to part with your $250,000 — or even a lesser figure — to become a contributor to the women's Final Four. It was, after all, a bit much to spend on basketball tickets.

At the end of 1999, according to Cathy Andruzzi, executive director of the local coordinating committee, PWB 2000 was still significantly shy of the nearly $2 million it hoped to spend on the tournament.

"We have about $600,000 to go. If I don't have it, I can't plan," she said. "It is Dec. 29, and I have to make some decisions. I know there are things we have to do and there are things we want to do."

In 1999, when the women's Final Four was in San Jose, Calif., that city's budget was $1.6 million. Among the big-ticket items were $80,000 for marketing the event and another $90,000 to decorate the San Jose Arena.

One difficulty encountered by both San Jose and Philadelphia was an NCAA rule preventing local organizing committees from directly soliciting funds from any of the NCAA's national contributors. Those contributors — national firms such as GTE — also were the only sponsors given advertising access to the interior of the First Union Center, where the games were played.

The most valuable commodities were the game tickets. Since the games were sold out, the only way to attend the tournament was by becoming a contributor or knowing one. "If this was the men's Final Four, I would be done fund-raising now," Andruzzi said.

While the PWB 2000 organizers dealt with fund-raising efforts, the first of what would become three meetings between the top programs in women's basketball was set to take place. Tennessee and Connecticut scheduled an unprecedented nonconference home-and-home series, first in Knoxville, Tenn., in early January, then in Storrs, Conn., to be followed by a meeting on the ultimate stage: in the national title game.

— *Christopher K. Hepp*

VICKI VALERIO / Inquirer Staff Photographer

Shea Ralph sparked Connecticut – and averted a steal by
Katie Davis – as the Huskies cruised past Villanova, 79-46.

The game everyone was waiting for was the first matchup between the two titans – UConn and Tennessee. That game was in Knoxville on the first Saturday of 2000.

Huskies Ready for Round 1

So just how good was the top-ranked Connecticut women's basketball team?

"I guess we're going to find out in Knoxville," coach Geno Auriemma said of the first confrontation with second-ranked Tennessee. "And if it doesn't work out, I guess we'll just come back home and fix it."

Both teams entered the game averaging more than 90 points per contest, and Huskies junior guard Shea Ralph had emerged as a leader after suffering various knee injuries in previous seasons.

"I'm very comfortable with my position on the team and very comfortable with my teammates," Ralph said. "We're all on the same page. It just feels different this year than in the past. We're clicking on the floor."

The series was scheduled as a made-for-TV event. Round 2 was scheduled for Feb. 2, on ESPN during part of its "Rivalry Week" prime-time package.

"A while ago, [ESPN] pointed out to me that the UCLA and Notre Dame men used to meet twice," Auriemma said. Eventually, he called Summitt about possibly scheduling an in-season home-and-home series. "She's good about that stuff, with national TV involved, exposure for the women's game," Auriemma said.

But he added: "If we start going 0-2, I don't think you'll see this [arrangement] last."

— *Mel Greenberg*

With home court such an advantage, the outcome was a surprise, and a foreshadowing of things to come.

Bird and UConn Ace the First Test

Top-ranked Connecticut survived the ultimate road test by beating No. 2 Tennessee, 74-67.

"Sometimes, in a game like this, there's so much pressure on the great players to do well that other guys usually step up," Auriemma said after the triumph in Knoxville. "That's what happened. Our other guys did more than their other guys."

One of them was sophomore point guard Sue Bird, who led the Huskies with 25 points. The graduate of Christ the King High in New York City also hit key baskets down the stretch when Tennessee was threatening. Connecticut got strong support from senior center Paige Sauer, who had not been much of a contributor in past meetings between the two national powers.

A year earlier, Bird was sidelined after suffering a knee injury early in Connecticut's schedule. The Volunteers beat the Huskies in Storrs, Conn. "It was a helpless feeling," Bird recalled. "There was nothing I could do. I wasn't even on the bench. It was killing me."

Tennessee coach Pat Summitt praised Bird's play. "When we were making a run, she was stepping up and making something happen," she said. "She was the difference. ... I'm not mad at my team; I'm just disappointed that they didn't play like they've been playing. But you have to give credit to Connecticut."

Tennessee suffered through the play of juniors Tamika Catchings and Kristen Clement, who didn't score a point in this game. "Tamika has to step up and make plays in this sit-

VICKI VALERIO / Inquirer Staff Photographer

Sue Bird was a key player for the Huskies in their first meeting with Tennessee. The sophomore point guard led the way with 25 points in a 74-67 victory in Knoxville.

uation," Summitt said. "Ace Clement today was not the Ace Clement we've been watching. The way [the Huskies] started the game, Ace was too tentative and didn't take charge for us. But she'll learn from this, because she's very coachable."

— *Mel Greenberg*

Summitt made a change at point guard shortly there-after, moving Clement to shooting guard and freshman Kara Lawson to the point. Meanwhile, like Tennessee, Connecticut made a regular-season appearance in Philadelphia, playing fellow Big East member Villanova on Jan. 23.

For Huskies, a Scouting Trip to Philly

In December, the Tennessee women's basketball team came to Philadelphia, played St. Joe's, checked out the town, and declared a definite desire to return. Real soon. In January, the team taking the tour was the mighty Connecticut Huskies, who, like Tennessee, made the first of two trips.

With apologies to Pat Summitt's Vols, UConn was the one team you could bank on seeing back in town when Philadelphia hosted its first Division I women's Final Four. "This," said Geno Auriemma, "is the first of three [victories in Philadelphia], we hope. It's hard not to think about it."

Philadelphia was already a favorite of the Huskies. Instead of scooting back to Storrs, they partook of the city's cuisine, tooled around like tourists, and even took in a Sixers game, for the Sixers' arena is where they wanted to be come April. In fact, it was where they fully expected to be.

"In 22 years, I just haven't seen a better team 1 through 10," Villanova coach Harry Perretta said. "Every time they

VICKI VALERIO / Inquirer Staff Photographer

Villanova coach Harry Perretta complained about a non-call, but UConn's Kennitra Johnson raced away after a steal. The deep Huskies flattened the Wildcats at the Pavilion.

sub, there's no change in the game. Every time they change, the pressure is the same, whether they're playing their first player or they're playing their eighth player."

Perretta knew of what he spoke. His Wildcats got drubbed by Connecticut, 79-46.

— *Claire Smith*

UConn's Muscle Overwhelms 'Nova

Villanova stayed within a point of unbeaten Connecticut through the first five minutes of the Big East contest at the Pavilion, but UConn, behind its constant pressure and deep bench, pulled away for a 79-46 triumph in front of a crowd of 4,059. The game marked the annual homecoming of Auriemma, who grew up in Norristown.

"A lot of these kids have never been here before," Auriemma said of his decision to take his team to the First Union Center after the game. "Usually, we're in and out."

Villanova's Perretta was philosophical after Connecticut had transformed the Pavilion into a 40-minute pressure cooker, forcing 17 turnovers. "I just thought it was a good game for our kids to play today," he said. "You're not going to see that kind of pressure too often during the season. I thought we handled it pretty well. Our goal was to try to beat the pressure, and if we couldn't get a layup, we were trying to get a three-point shot. That was our [approach]."

The Huskies' balance showed in the scoring. Swin Cash and Shea Ralph each scored 13 points, while Sue Bird and Svetlana Abrosimova both scored 12. "We're good, but we can get better," Ralph said.

— *Mel Greenberg*

A week later, Connecticut hosted Round 2 of its series with Tennessee. After winning Round 1, Auriemma dismissed talk of pressure to sweep the Vols. "I don't think anything bad happened to them after we beat them down there, and I don't think they gave us the national championship," he said.

Maybe not, but there were aftereffects. The

Huskies solidified their position at the top of the polls. Tennessee, meanwhile, struggled at home two days later before beating Arkansas and then was pounded, 78-51, at Georgia, a Southeastern Conference rival. But then Kara Lawson solidified herself at the point, especially after scoring 22 points in Tennessee's win over Kentucky.

While play at point guard attracted the attention when the teams first met, Auriemma expected the inside game to be a key in the second contest. "Last time, it was Sue [Bird] and Svet [Abrosimova]," he said. "We need help from a couple of other players."

In Round 2, Vols Knock Off No. 1

Tennessee junior Semeka Randall cut the heart out of Connecticut with two last-minute dagger shots, one with four seconds left, to give the fourth-ranked Volunteers a 72-71 victory over the top-ranked and previously unbeaten Huskies at Gampel Pavilion.

The Huskies still had a chance to triumph, but Tamika Williams' last-second shot hit the underside of the rim as the buzzer sounded.

There appeared to be body contact from Tennessee's Michelle Snow on the play, but no foul was called.

"In that situation, it's a no-call," Williams said after her team fell to 19-1. "I have to take [the ball] up stronger. ... You've got to live with it."

The triumph in Storrs, Conn., gave a measure of revenge to Tennessee (17-3), setting up a third and deciding meeting between the two for the ultimate prize — the NCAA championship — on April 2 at the First Union Center.

"I got a good look and just took the shot," Randall said of her game-winner. "I didn't think twice about it. I just went with my instincts, and my instincts told me to shoot it. And it went in."

Randall also hit a shot with 27 seconds left, but Sue Bird, the heroine of the Connecticut victory in Knoxville, got the lead back for the Huskies on a jumper with 17 seconds left.

Tamika Catchings led Tennessee with 19 points and 13 rebounds, while Randall had 17 points. Snow had 13.

Connecticut was led by Williams' 19 points, while Shea Ralph had 16, Bird 15, and Svetlana Abrosimova 11.

It took a long while for this game to cook in what has become a heated rivalry since the series began in 1995. The drama didn't build until Connecticut began to rally from a 63-54 deficit with 7 minutes, 17 seconds to play.

Williams carried the Huskies with nine points in the comeback, including a three-point play that gave Connecticut a 66-65 lead with 3 minutes, 44 seconds remaining.

The lead then changed sides twice until the first of Randall's two game-breaking jump shots.

"It's fitting it came down to the last shot," Auriemma said. "It was an odd game to be involved in. It looked like there were a lot of games within the game: the first 17 minutes, the next 17 minutes, the last six minutes."

— *Mel Greenberg*

A little more than a week later, Connecticut went to Rutgers, which was gaining momentum as the regular season climbed toward its zenith. Rutgers was led by Shawnetta Stewart, a Philadelphia product. First, a look at her path.

The Scarlet Knights' Shining Star

It is usually never a good thing to wind up right where you started. Not so for Shawnetta Stewart.

The basketball player who had trouble escaping Philadelphia, and the stigma of a floundering public school system, wanted back in, desperately. Philadelphia is the place where Stewart, the centerpiece of the Rutgers women's basketball team, not only began and ended a storied high school career. It is also the place where Stewart wanted to have her college career culminate, because Philadelphia was home to the women's Final Four.

Envisioning Stewart cutting down the net after a national championship was a long shot. After all, Rutgers still existed in the long shadow of Connecticut and other monster programs. But being a long shot was what Stewart — and the Rutgers team that followed her lead for three seasons — was all about.

Rutgers dotted the national rankings all season because the 5-foot-10 guard/forward proved worthy of the "Total Package" nickname she carried, leading the Knights in scoring (15.3 points per game) and rebounding (6.5) entering the UConn game.

Stewart had to fight for the privilege of doing it all from the very start. Proposition 48 students, as they are branded and condemned, aren't supposed to have it easy. Their lives don't revolve around country-club dances, leased SUVs, weekends at the Hamptons, or ski trips to Vail. Their time is occupied more often by trying to get through broken school systems and the piranha-filled basketball backwaters.

Stewart survived University City without ever flunking a class, only to nearly fall through the net during the

VICKI VALERIO / Inquirer Staff Photographer

Coach Vivian Stringer stood and watched nervously as her
Scarlet Knights scrapped with Notre Dame in the semifinals of
the Big East tournament. Rutgers prevailed, 81-72, in overtime.

recruiting wars because of her Scholastic Assessment Test scores. "She didn't have a good foundation," said Stewart's mother, Arnetta.

Stewart was lucky, though. She was not condemned to oblivion by a system that failed her. Plenty of schools wanted the talent that had surpassed Wilt Chamberlain's Philadelphia high-school scoring record. More than one agreed to assume the burden of building a college-caliber student first before building an all-American-caliber college player.

But Stewart chose Rutgers because of its coach, Vivian Stringer. Stringer, like her mentor, John Chaney, refuses to believe that there is a socioeconomic cutoff when it comes to affording education to students. New to Rutgers, Stringer, long familiar with the player known in Philadelphia as "The Baby Barkley" as well as the person, knew Stewart could help her build a winner.

Stringer also believed she could help Stewart succeed off the court. So she recruited the player as if she had cruised through the preppiest of prep schools.

"Shawnetta didn't want to go to a school that was rebuilding, but she and Coach bonded," Arnetta Stewart said.

A challenge was implied from the outset. Not only would Stewart have to go to school for a year and major in academics as opposed to basketball. But Arnetta Stewart, a single mother, would have to pay for that freshman experience, and Shawnetta would have to earn grades good enough to assure three years of academic eligibility.

She did.

"She's a 3.0 this semester and a high-C throughout," Arnetta Stewart said. "It's been difficult at times. That first year, there was a rumor that she flunked out. I think people expected her to."

It was then that Stewart heard her mother's pleading words. "She needed to rethink her education," Arnetta Stewart said. "I told her to never let anyone tell her what she cannot accomplish."

Three years later, the Stewarts saw graduation on the horizon. Shawnetta needed one semester beyond her senior season and planned to complete that in the fall, since she intended to be busy during the summer — playing, she hoped, in the WNBA.

"But she will graduate," her mother promised. "She's going to get a degree. She worked too hard in the beginning for all of this to have been in vain."

The basketball career hasn't been in vain, either. Rutgers is very much on the map, because Stewart put it there, leading the Knights into the Sweet 16 as a sophomore and the Elite Eight as a junior. In her senior season, the Final Four was the goal.

— *Claire Smith*

Stewart scored 13 against Connecticut. But it wasn't enough.

Rutgers Defense Dazzles; UConn Wins

Top-ranked Connecticut's offensive scoring machine spent most of Feb. 12 spinning its wheels against the tenacious defense of 10th-ranked Rutgers. Eventually, however, the Huskies rolled with an 8-0 run late in the second half, and emerged with a 49-45 victory in a Big East women's basketball game at the Louis Brown Athletic Center.

It was the lowest point total for Connecticut since the Huskies lost to Villanova, 50-44, in January 1993. The visit-

VICKI VALERIO / Inquirer Staff Photographer

Connecticut's players rejoiced after the Huskies finished off
Rutgers, 79-59, to capture the Big East Conference championship.

ing Huskies entered the game averaging 85.5 points per game. "The only thing that we might have done well is win the game," Auriemma said after his team rallied against Rutgers for the second time in the 1999-2000 season. "I always worry after we have two good practices, and Thursday and Friday were the two best ones we've had all year."

— *Mel Greenberg*

As March neared, Philadelphia Women's Basketball 2000 still lacked full funding to host the Final Four. Cathy Andruzzi turned to the city and the state, after securing a few more corporate sponsors, including the 76ers.

The Final Fund-Raising Push

Cathy Andruzzi admitted that fund-raising for PWB 2000 had been "hairy," but if Mayor Street and the state of Pennsylvania accepted her proposals, the local coordinating committee for the women's Final Four would be in what she described as a financial comfort zone. The organization was about $500,000 shy of its $1.4 million fund-raising goal.

"We've had a good relationship with them, and we know they're going to come through for us," Andruzzi said of the city's and state's decision-makers. "This has great economic impact on both the state and the city. The mayor is really into fitness, and he knows we want to encourage fitness, so we're right in line with that.

"If this had been the men's Final Four, we'd be done by now," Andruzzi said.

— *Ashley McGeachy*

*In the preseason, Rutgers had been proclaimed the
team to beat in the Big East Conference, but doubts
arose when the host Scarlet Knights dropped a 66-65
overtime loss to Villanova early in the season. Vivian
Stringer's Knights got their chance at revenge on Feb.
27.*

Rutgers Makes a Statement

Eighth-ranked Rutgers took a simple approach at the
Pavilion to avenging the Villanova nightmare: Just put the
ball in the basket. Stringer's group did that effectively in
the second half with a 19-for-24 effort that led to a 76-60
Big East victory in the regular-season conference finale.

Said Villanova's Harry Perretta: "The first time we
played them, when they missed a few shots early in the
game, they would hesitate to take shots. Now they just continue to play. They don't hesitate, and that's a big factor
and mind-set in scoring."

"This is a new day," Stringer said. "The cylinders are
beginning to click, but I'm still not willing to say we're
peaking. But it certainly makes us feel good."

The Scarlet Knights finished tied with Boston College
in the standings but broke the deadlock because of their
win over the Eagles a week earlier.

"You know, when you look back [at the season] now,"
Stringer said, "it was all about positioning. That's what the
27 games mean. But now we all start anew. We're so close,
I can smell it. We're beginning to taste it."

— *Mel Greenberg*

REBECCA BARGER-TUVIM / Inquirer Staff Photographer

St. Joseph's coach Stephanie Gaitley watched a large-screen television and talked on her cellular phone as the Hawks awaited their NCAA tournament seeding at the First Union Center. St. Joseph's was seeded 10th in the West, which put it on a collision course with Rutgers.

Chapter 3

The Chosen Ones

Connecticut won another Big East tournament title, and Tennessee came from behind to beat Mississippi State in the Southeastern Conference championship game. Rutgers finished second to UConn in the Big East tournament, and Penn State was upset by Purdue. Yet they all drew high seedings in the 64-team NCAA tournament, the Vols and Huskies No. 1 seeds, and the Scarlet Knights and Nittany Lions No. 2. The dance was on.

For Auriemma, the seeding was another step toward his home.

There's No Hiding Auriemma's Success

For Donato Auriemma, a Norristown factory worker who made cinder blocks and candy and never learned English, life's highs and lows took place behind closed doors.

Whenever the Italian immigrant's eyes got moist — at weddings, funerals or on the night his son's basketball team won a national championship — he excused himself. Men worked. Earned. Disciplined. They did not cry.

"My father," said Geno Auriemma, the University of Connecticut's women's basketball coach, "was in the bathroom for a lot of life's great moments."

And though Donato Auriemma's son has an NCAA championship trophy on his desk and a photo of him with President Clinton on an office wall, he too finds the need to retreat to the quiet side of a closed door.

"The more attention this team gets, the more uncomfortable I am. I retreat into here a little more," Auriemma said as he wolfed down pasta and vegetables in his office.

"Phil [Martelli, the St. Joseph's men's coach who is a close friend] knows the janitor, the cleaning woman, everybody in his building. I wish I could be like that. When I was younger and first got the job here, I tried really hard to be like that. And I was for a while. But as things grew and grew, I found myself hiding in my office more."

Trim and wavy-haired at 45, with a swagger and accent that betray his Philadelphia-area roots, Auriemma ought to be riding the Husky-mania wave that has washed over this compact state like a blue-and-white tsunami in the last decade. Four days earlier, Connecticut had thumped Tennessee in Knoxville.

Instead, he seems to be watching it all from a distance. Happy with his team's excellence and happy with his own success (with a $248,000 salary that is supplemented by camp and Nike money), Auriemma wishes that he, like the Wizard of Oz, could do it all from behind a curtain.

"I remember coming back from Minneapolis [after Connecticut's 35-0 season in 1994-95 concluded with a national championship]," he said. "The first thing I asked our [athletic director] on the plane was, 'Is there any way

JERRY LODRIGUSS / Inquirer Staff Photographer

Geno Auriemma enjoyed the closing seconds of an 86-71 triumph over Louisiana State. The victory in the East Regional final punched UConn's ticket to the Final Four.

we can do what we just did and not have to deal with what's coming next?' And he said, 'No, I'm sorry.'

"There's a price to pay," Auriemma said. "You go to your kids' games and wear a baseball hat and hope no one recognizes you. You go shopping to buy a book and everybody wants to talk about last night's game. People want to give you all this money to do commercials. I've got a TV show, a radio show. All of a sudden you say, 'Wait a minute, this can't be right. There's too much going on.' "

The pressure to win and sell tickets has grown like the game itself in women's basketball. When Auriemma arrived in Storrs in 1985, Connecticut's women had never been to an NCAA tourney and drew a few hundred fans to their games. Now they sell out Gampel Pavilion with fans who don't understand — or accept — losses.

"In Oklahoma last month, a guy said, 'Don't you guys ever have a bad year?' I said we did. And he said, 'What's a bad year in Connecticut?' I said, 'If we don't win the national championship, that's a bad year.' You laugh, but that's the way it is. It's like coaching the Yankees."

Whatever happens, it's not going to measure up to those Friday nights when Auriemma was a boys' basketball assistant to Martelli at his alma mater, Norristown's old Bishop Kenrick High School.

Then, after Kenrick's games, the two of them, with $10 or $20 in their wallets, would go out for beer and steamers at the Glass Rack bar. They'd talk about basketball and life. Go home broke and happy. And no one ever interrupted for an autograph.

"It was the most fun I ever remember," he said. "You don't want to go back to those days ... but now, with all this craziness up here, you hope that you can kind of hold on to those memories. It's kind of what keeps me going when you lose to Tennessee and everyone is going to have a heart attack and you have to answer questions about what's wrong with your team for two weeks. Guys like [Villanova women's coach] Harry Perretta look at me and think one of two things. It's either, 'Boy, he's got it made.' Or, 'Man I wouldn't want that life.' "

Auriemma wrestles constantly with that dichotomy. There are days when he is convinced he is the luckiest man in America, coaching a dominant team that has remained scandal-free.

But there are other days, like this one, when the opponent is a pushover and he clearly is in conflict with himself. The postgame beer and steamers have been replaced by more demands and more questions.

During 14-plus seasons in the rocky and remote New England town of Storrs, Auriemma has turned a team that perennially finished last in the Big East into a national powerhouse. His teams have won nine Big East titles, made four Final Four trips and captured NCAA titles in '95 and 2000.

He has done it by being tough, foul-mouthed, brusque and unconcerned with his critics, many of them female coaches who dislike his harsh tactics and are convinced that he looks down his nose at them. He thumbed that same nose at tradition in 1998 when, during a game at Villanova, he and Perretta contrived a way for injured Huskies star Nykesha Sales to reach a scoring milestone.

"I've never really been politically correct," he said. "I've gotten in trouble for some things, but I really don't give a [hoot]. A lot of women that coach women's basketball approach it like it's women's basketball. I don't. I approach it like it's basketball. I make the same demands of my players as if I were coaching men. I don't compro-

When Geno Auriemma comes home, he enjoys visiting with his cousins, Sal and Yvonne Auriemma, in South Philadelphia. The siblings watched passersby outside their store, Claudio's King of Cheese.

mise one bit.

"I get all kind of letters. ... That's because the girls are nice and smile a lot and they're pretty. They don't know what a pain in the butt they are to coach. They're 18, 19, 20, and you treat them as such. I've been lucky. I get the kind of kids that want to be treated that way."

And he and Jim Calhoun, the coach of Connecticut's defending national champion men's basketball team — whom Auriemma, nodding his head toward Calhoun's adjacent office, called the "problem next door" — have, at best, a strained relationship.

When UConn comes to town, Auriemma takes his team

to South Philly for cheesesteaks and a visit to his cousin's Ninth Street cheese shop. He still refers reverently to past Big Five coaches, and gets goose bumps recalling the first time he brought a team into the Palestra.

"He talks about Philly all the time. It's Philly this and Philly that," said AnnMarie Person, UConn's assistant director of athletic communications.

Auriemma remains at heart a Philadelphian. He is cocky, loquacious, street-smart and, most of all, convinced that good fortune is only a temporary condition. As secure as any coach in the nation, he can't always shake the fear that a single loss might leave him unemployed.

"I used to think I had to win every game to prove I can coach," he said. "If I lost a game, it meant I can't coach. That's from Philly. Philly coaches think they can take four donkeys and win the Kentucky Derby.

"Philly teams were always big underdogs. You had people coming into the Palestra strutting their [stuff], and these guys would find a way to knock them off. But then you go and watch the ACC, watch Duke and North Carolina, and you realize that it's about the players. So while I've moved away from that winning-all-the-time stuff, a part of me still believes it."

Donato Auriemma, who brought his wife and 7-year-old son here from Montella, Italy, in 1961, worked tirelessly in America — first at a Conshohocken candy plant and then at a cinder-block manufacturer in Norristown. But he never took a paycheck for granted.

"My father came up when I bought my second house here [in Manchester, Conn.]," recalled Auriemma. "He looked around the big place and he said, 'How you going to pay for all this?' I said, 'What do you mean? I get paid.' And he said, 'What happens if there are no more games?' "

He has helped make UConn the poster child for women's athletics. Huskies attendance for the last six years is the nation's best, though Tennessee has moved into a bigger arena and has been drawing bigger numbers recently. TV and radio ratings for the women's games are phenomenal in Connecticut. When the Huskies played the Vols, the Nielsen rating for the game in the Hartford area was nearly twice as high as that for the NFL playoff game between Washington and Detroit.

The team's graduation rate is 100 percent, and a whole new generation of girls has grown up with pictures of Huskies stars, such as Sales and Rebecca Lobo, on their bedroom walls.

Yet for all that success, Auriemma still believes he'll never be as good as his high school coach at Kenrick, Buddy Gardler.

"I wanted to be like him," Auriemma said of Gardler, now coaching at Cardinal O'Hara. "I wanted to teach like him. I wanted to be looked at the way we looked at him. He played for [Jack] Ramsay. He played at St. Joe's. It was like, 'You're God. And you're teaching us to play basketball?' "

━━━━━━

Auriemma had been born Luigi Auriemma in Montella, near Naples, in 1954. When he was 7, his parents emigrated to join relatives working at Alan Wood Steel in the Conshohocken area.

"My mother tells me there was one basketball hoop in our little town in Italy and that when I was little I would go there and watch them play," he said.

The Auriemmas moved in with relatives across the street from Lincoln Elementary School. Geno played basketball on the playground, but it was baseball that captivated him immediately.

It wasn't until his sophomore year at Kenrick that he made the basketball team. And at his very first practice with Gardler, something clicked.

"I got hooked on basketball right then," he said. "It really hit me that this was something I really enjoyed. I understood what Buddy was teaching us. I could see what he was trying to do."

As a player, a guard, he was borderline Big Five material.

"Paul Westhead was at La Salle and Jack McKinney was at St. Joe's. They said I could play freshman there, but there was no guarantee I'd make the varsity," Auriemma said. "I thought to myself, 'I'm not good enough to play at those places.' Now if my parents had spoken English and gone to high school and college here, they probably would have said, 'Look, we don't care if you play or not, if you have a chance to go to those schools, you're going.'"

Auriemma knew he could play at nearby Montgomery County Community College. He met his wife, Kathy, there, worked at a number of jobs, and eventually transferred to West Chester.

It was then, in the mid-1970s, when an old Kenrick teammate, Jim Foster, telephoned him.

"He was at Temple, and out of the blue he calls and says, 'Hey, I'm coaching the girls at Bishop McDevitt. You want to help me?'" said Auriemma. "I said, 'No way. I wouldn't coach girls for all the money in the world.' When I was at Kenrick, we wouldn't even let the girls on the court."

Foster finally convinced him. Auriemma had grown up with his own preconceptions of what girls could and couldn't do athletically. But he determined from the start that he would teach them just as Gardler had coached the boys.

VICKI VALERIO / Inquirer Staff Photographer

On a physical play under the basket, Connecticut's Kelly Schumacher (11) was fouled by Boston College's Becky Gottstein. The Huskies rolled to a 79-54 win in the Big East semifinals.

Twenty-five years later, he still does.

"Obviously, their skill levels are very different from men," he said. "Sometimes we'll run a play perfectly and the kid will hit the bottom of the rim with a layup. And I'll say, 'If I was coaching guys, that would have been a dunk.'

"But deep down inside, and that's what people don't get, these women want what the guys want. They want to be challenged. They want to be pushed. They want to be told, 'This is right; this is wrong.' They would be offended if you said to a guy, 'That's unacceptable,' but said to them, 'That's OK, I understand. We're going to do it a little different for you because I don't want you to break a nail.' "

After two years at McDevitt, Foster, now Vanderbilt's coach, got the St. Joseph's women's job and brought Auriemma along. The only problem was his salary. He was making $1,000 a year.

"I said, 'This isn't going anywhere. I've got to get a real job,' " he recalled.

By 1979, Gardler had left Kenrick for Cardinal O'Hara High and Martelli had replaced him.

He hired Auriemma as his assistant.

"I thought, 'Wow, what a break. I'm coaching boys at my old high school. This is it. Down the road, I'm going to be Jimmy Lynam.' ... They were two of the best years of my life. Playing in those little gyms. Riding the buses back from Bishop Egan or some God-forsaken place. ... But eventually, I saw that the teachers there made only $15,000 a year."

Martelli worked at the summer camps of Immaculata's Cathy Rush, one of the pioneers of women's basketball. The best college coaches attended. In 1981, Martelli told Auriemma that Virginia coach Debbie Ryan was looking for a full-time assistant.

"I thought, 'Man, I don't want to go that women's route again.' But I went down and looked. It was my first time out of Philly. I thought all colleges looked like Temple or St. Joe's. Then I saw that beautiful campus. They had Ralph Sampson and their men were No. 1 in the country. I said, 'Holy s---!' And I signed on the spot."

He spent four years there and had a couple of offers that didn't work out. In 1985, having heard of the opening through the Philadelphia coaching network, Auriemma interviewed to replace Connecticut's Jean Balthaser, who had had four straight nine-win seasons.

"I know I wasn't their first choice, but I got the job in May," he said. "We won our first seven games, and I thought, 'Here we go.' Then we lost like nine straight."

He recruited Kerry Bascom, and things improved. The Huskies made their first NCAA appearance in 1989. By 1991, Bascom's senior season, they reached the Final Four and were playing in a new arena.

"We averaged maybe 800 to 1,000 people," he said. "Then that November, we signed Rebecca Lobo, the number-one prospect in the country. Now, all of a sudden, everybody loves us. We're the darlings. Our attendance goes up to 3,000 a game. In her junior year, we beat Auburn at Auburn and beat Virginia here. All hell broke loose. From that day on, the games have been on TV and you can't get a ticket."

Connecticut's women's games attract a far different crowd than the Huskies men — families and thousands of young girls.

"There's only one group of people our game hasn't captured," said Auriemma. "The 21-to-30-year-old single guy who wants to go to dinner with three buddies, drink a couple of beers, go to the game and [curse] the ref. We haven't captured the guy who spits on Charles Barkley. And that's the guy the other sports are aimed at. But we've got everyone else."

If Auriemma sounds defensive, he is. He knows that for all its growth and success, women's basketball continues to be viewed as a second-rate freak show by many. That animosity surfaced after the Sales incident.

Sales had suffered a career-ending injury two points shy of Bascom's Connecticut scoring record. She was one of her coach's favorites, and Auriemma sought a solution. Comfortable with Perretta, he called the Villanova coach a few days before their Feb. 24 game there.

"The funny thing was, before I could ask Harry, he said to me, 'How can we do this?' " said Auriemma.

They agreed that the injured Sales and a Villanova player would exchange uncontested baskets at the start of the game. The reaction was immediate and furious. Critics blasted him for tampering with the integrity of the game and further trivializing women's sports.

"You had guys who had never watched a women's game in their lives saying I was screwing with the game," said Auriemma, whose father had died earlier that season. "After the kid made the basket, the 4,000 people in the place went crazy, standing on their feet and cheering. Then we picked up the papers and read how we were real [jerks] for acting that way.

"It was like, 'Here's our chance to take a shot at women's basketball. They think they're so hot, so clean, so cute. They're good students, they don't have the problems the men do, the money, the agents. We can't have this.' So a lot of guys living in caves came out."

Now, with the advent of the WNBA, and the realization among college administrators that women's sports can make money, the women's game seems to be losing its innocence. (Connecticut's women's basketball team generated a $2 million profit in 1998-99, Auriemma said.)

"It's sad," he said. "Women's coaches are demanding the same pay as men, and they're being put under the same pressures. They get fired if they don't win. So to save your job, you pull a few strings here and there, admit a kid you wouldn't have before.

"We're dealing with some things the men's game has suffered through," he said. "And a lot of these women, they want to be like the men. That's the worst thing that could ever happen. The men are the men. If you try to be like them, there's no reason to watch because you can't be that good. Stay unique. Carve out a little niche for yourselves."

In 1999, when the Connecticut men won the NCAA title, the testy relationship between Auriemma and Calhoun bobbed to the surface. Calhoun preferred not to discuss it, but people in Storrs insist he and Auriemma wage a constant fight for the spotlight. And Auriemma felt the men's coach ignored him.

"I've got a problem next door, but everybody has one of those," said Auriemma. "You could trade him for something worse. I was spoiled because I had Jimmy Lynam [at St. Joe's] and Terry Holland [at Virginia]. Guys that took you on their charter, took you out to dinner."

Auriemma insists he has no desire to make the move to the men's game or the WNBA, where he has been an analyst on telecasts. The only thing that could drive him away, he said, was if the mounting pressure spiraled out of control.

Until then, he'll close the door to his office whenever possible and daydream.

"You know what my dream job would be?" he asked,

rising from his chair and preparing to do his TV and radio shows. "If, when my kids [two teenage daughters and a son in fifth grade] are older, Martelli wins the Atlantic Ten and the NCAA title and gets the Sixers job. I'd like to be his assistant.

"I wouldn't scout or travel. I'd just go to practice every day and work with the guys. I'd have come full circle. That would be ideal."

— *Frank Fitzpatrick*

For Penn State, the NCAA tournament meant a chance to take another step. In 1997, the Nittany Lions watched the Final Four. In '98, they won the Women's NIT. In '99, there was a Sweet 16 appearance. In 2000, their goal was higher.

Penn State Chases Its Ultimate Dream

They walked through downtown Cincinnati, awed by the fervor surrounding the 1997 women's Final Four. After a tumultuous 15-13 season, seven Lions underclassmen piled into two cars and drove eight hours for this glimpse of glory.

ESPN analyst Robin Roberts lounged in a hotel lobby, not far from Connecticut all-American Rebecca Lobo. Banners hung from skyscrapers as ticket scalpers scurried for top dollar to the sold-out event. Bands played. Inside the arena, fans with faces painted cheered as Tennessee won the second of its three consecutive national titles.

They saw it all, from the spectators' perspective. Three years later, after winning the Big Ten regular-season title and posting a 26-4 record, the Lions wanted to see it from the players' perspective. They wanted to finish the season

VICKI VALERIO / Inquirer Staff Photographer

Rene Portland coached Penn State to an 83-63 victory over Youngstown State in the NCAA tournament. The Lions rattled off three more wins to make the Final Four.

in Philadelphia.

"In Cincinnati, we saw everybody we didn't think we'd ever see or meet in person," said Andrea Garner, a Philadelphia native and a first-team all-Big Ten selection in 1999-2000. "Seeing all those people walking around, it was like, 'Wow.' Now that we're in that position to be the ones that people are looking at ... it's exciting."

Two weeks and four games were all that stood between the Lions, seeded second in the Midwest, and Philadelphia.

That Penn State and the Final Four were spoken in the same breath was unthinkable when Garner, Helen Darling and the other Lions made that trek to Cincinnati. Penn State finished tied for sixth in the Big Ten that year, which meant no NCAA tournament bid for just the second time in school history.

Frustrated, Garner and Darling talked about transferring. They didn't, and as sophomores, they finished seventh in the Big Ten. Reluctantly, the Lions accepted a bid to the Women's National Invitation Tournament, which Garner sarcastically called the "Not-In Tournament."

Cognizant of her team's indifference, coach Rene Portland threatened to pull out of the event, but instead the Lions swept Villanova, St. Joseph's and Indiana by an average of 16 points before beating Baylor for the WNIT title.

"That helped lay the foundation," Portland said.

The 1998-99 season was another step. Penn State finished second in the Big Ten and, after getting a disappointingly low seed, upset Virginia before losing to Louisiana Tech in the second round of the NCAA tournament.

When the Lions got home from Ruston, La., Portland met with the players. They set goals for the next season, goals that were posted on the locker-room door inside the Bryce Jordan Center:

Go undefeated in nonconference competition at home. The Lions did, beating Villanova, St. Francis (Pa.), then-sixth-ranked Auburn, Pittsburgh and Florida.

Break into the top 10 by Christmas. After starting the season at No. 10 but falling to No. 12, Penn State rose to No. 6 after the Auburn win, more than a week before the holiday.

Win the Big Ten regular-season title.

Draw a top-16 seed in the NCAA tournament.

And the last three goals: Reach the Elite Eight, go to Philly, take pictures with President Clinton at the White House.

One goal not reached was winning the Big Ten tournament. The Lions lost in the championship game to Purdue, 71-63.

"I guess the NCAA tournament is the rubber match," Portland said.

To reach Philadelphia, where Portland won three national titles as a player at Immaculata in the 1970s, the Lions needed to play stingy defense, rebound better than they did in the Big Ten title game, and stay mentally strong, Portland said.

During the regular season, Penn State led the Big Ten in scoring (77 points per game), scoring defense (57.7), three-point shooting (36.8 percent), rebounding (42.5 per game), assists (19.4), and steals (11.3). Darling, the Big Ten player of the year, led the league in assists with 7.6 per game, while Garner ranked 10th in scoring (14.9 ppg.), second in rebounding (8.9 per game), and first in blocks (2.2).

Darling and Garner had been to a Final Four as spectators. Now they wanted to play in one.

"It would be a great way to end my career here, with everybody watching me who's watched me since I was a kid," Garner said. "Just to have people watch and say, 'I knew her,' or 'I played with her,' that'd be something I'd really enjoy."

Added Darling: "I really thought going to Cincinnati was a great idea. Let's go see how it feels. Let's go see the atmosphere, just so we would know how it feels. I think it gave us some drive. The Final Four was neat, and people there told us, 'When you make it to the Final Four they size you up for your rings.' Rings. Rings just sound so nice."

— *Ashley McGeachy*

Rutgers was supposed to get a high seeding, and the Scarlet Knights did. But getting to Philly was more difficult than forecast.

A Smooth Road for Rutgers?

Considering the potholes the Rutgers women's basketball team managed to hit between November and the announcement of the 64-team NCAA tournament field, the Scarlet Knights (22-7) could have fared worse with the selection committee.

Connecticut and Tennessee were sent elsewhere and did not stand as regional barriers to the dream that coach Vivian Stringer and senior Shawnetta Stewart had of making a homecoming appearance in the women's Final Four at the First Union Center.

But while the Scarlet Knights did get a lift as a home team with the No. 2 seed in the West, they also had some long-distance travel ahead of them.

However, home court was in Rutgers' favor in the tourney's opening weekend, an intangible that proved useful in a subregional mix that included St. Joseph's (24-5) and Texas (21-12).

The Scarlet Knights opened against Holy Cross (23-6), the Patriot League winner, after 10th-seeded St. Joseph's and seventh-seeded Texas squared off. The West subregional's winner would earn a trip to Portland, Ore.

"We are happy to be a No. 2 seed," Stringer said, "because I think we worked extremely hard during the season to position ourselves for this day. Our ultimate goal is to return to the East and to play in ... Philadelphia. We know we have a tremendous amount of work to do to get there."

Rutgers beat Texas by 68-64 in Piscataway, N.J., in December.

"We know what Texas is all about. But to see them beat Texas Tech, as you saw they did, it tells you they are a lot stronger than ever," Stringer said.

As for St. Joseph's, Stringer was full of compliments.

"St. Joe's will stun some people in here," she said. "They're the same team we met a couple of years ago just before Christmas, and we thought we could get that win and walk out of there.

"They stunned us then. Their coach [Stephanie Gaitley] has got those kids playing extremely hard and playing great defense. They are a group of hard-nosed players."

Stringer believed her Knights had recovered from the whipping Connecticut gave them in the Big East title game.

"It adds fuel to your fire more than anything else," Stringer said. "Connecticut was responsible for our poor play [in Hartford] to some extent, but we, on the other hand, came out and played very shaky from the beginning.

I think that our group will respond well to this."

— *Mel Greenberg*

And then there was Summitt's Tennessee team, which had survived another season under her thumb.

Tennessee's Titan: Pat Summitt

"Michelle!"

The moment Pat Summitt's fierce rebuke split the morning air, everything on the floor of the University of Tennessee's Thompson-Boling Arena ground to a sudden, silent and total halt. The most successful, celebrated and intimidating coach in all of women's college basketball was about to have a word with one of her players.

"Michelle!" Summitt growled again as Michelle Snow, the rail-thin, 6-foot-5 sophomore center for the Volunteers, froze in her tracks.

Five minutes earlier, Snow carried herself with the grace and dignity of a queen. No doubt she would again five minutes later. But for now, oh, man, Snow had the hangdog look of somebody who knew it was coming.

"We have been working on this play for 15 minutes," Summitt began, tearing into Snow as her voice and, it would seem, her blood pressure rose with each progressive word. "Why? Because one player won't commit to a system."

Snow, a Miss Basketball coming out of high school in Pensacola, Fla., two years before and, like virtually every starter for the Volunteers, a high school all-American, stood silently. As any player who has ever worn the Tennessee orange during Summitt's 26 years can testify, that's about all there is to do when Coach is lowering the boom. If you want to continue being part of a basketball dynasty, you stand there and take it and whisper to yourself: She's yelling at me because she wants me to be the best I can be. She's yelling at me because she wants the team to win. She's yelling at me because she loves me.

Summitt wasn't finished with Snow just yet. She pointed to the rafters, where six NCAA national championship banners hang — banners Summitt put there.

"You don't have one of those, do you?" she growled.

Snow's eyes — every player's eyes — turned toward the rafters, to the impressive and imposing reminders of Summitt's winning formula.

"No, you don't," Summitt snapped at Snow. "But you want one, don't you?"

Point made. Not just with Snow but with every Vol on the court.

"All right, then," said Summitt, much calmer now, almost tender. "Now, let's get this thing right."

═══════

Summitt, 47, is, by most any measure, the most successful coach in women's basketball. You want the list of college coaches, man or woman, men's basketball or women's, who have won more NCAA championships than Summitt? Here it is:

John Wooden.

Only the Wizard of Westwood, who built a dynasty at UCLA around the likes of Kareem Abdul-Jabbar and Bill Walton, has more titles, 10. Summitt has six NCAA championships, two more than Kentucky's legendary Adolph Rupp and three more than Indiana's Bobby Knight. Six NCAA titles are impressive enough, but they become even more so when you consider that all had come in the last 13 years, including an unprecedented three consecutive titles in 1995-96, 1996-97 and 1997-98.

When her teams didn't win the national championship, it wasn't as if they were out of contention. Summitt has led the Vols to the Final Four 16 times in the last 24 years, and 10 times in the last 15 years. Five times the Vols finished second.

Her winning percentage is equally eye-popping. Coming into the 1999-2000 campaign, Summitt's record was 695-146, meaning she had come out on top 82.6 percent of the time. (Her record as a coach in international competition is even better: 63-4, for 94 percent.) In raw number of wins, Summitt trailed only Texas'

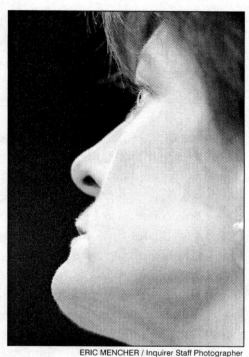

ERIC MENCHER / Inquirer Staff Photographer

Coach Pat Summitt was the picture of concentration as Tennessee practiced at the First Union Center. The Vols responded by beating Rutgers, 64-54.

Jody Conradt, who had been coaching six years longer. Along the way, Summitt had produced 10 U.S. Olympians and 16 Kodak all-Americans, and sent 22 players to the pros.

Her 1997-98 team, which went 39-0, won the NCAA

championship, and dominated opponents with an average margin of victory of 30.1 points, has been widely proclaimed as the greatest collegiate women's basketball team of all time.

Summitt's awards, honors and distinctions are far too numerous to list, except to note that she was enshrined in June 1999 in the Women's Basketball Hall of Fame and that she had been nominated for the Class of 2000 for the Basketball Hall of Fame in Springfield, Mass.

And the thing is, Summitt is nowhere near ready to call it quits.

"I've got the fire right now just as much as I had in my first year of coaching," Summitt, relaxing in her comfortable office at Thompson-Boling, said after a practice.

This from a woman who never set out to be a coach. A former college star at Tennessee-Martin, she was a farm girl who expected to become a schoolteacher and move home to Ashland City, Tenn., to marry and raise a family. But she was working as a graduate assistant for the Vols' basketball team when the head coach unexpectedly quit. When she was offered the job, she figured she'd give it a try.

Close to three decades later, she was married to a bank president, the mother of a 9-year-old son, and one of the most famous people in all of Tennessee.

It's all enough to spook many opposing coaches, some of whom are as awed and intimidated by Summitt as their players are of her teams. Stephanie Gaitley, coach of St. Joseph's, recalled a trip to Knoxville a year before, when the Hawks were catching Tennessee in the first game after Purdue had unexpectedly halted the defending national champion's 46-game winning streak.

"We sort of felt the brunt of that loss," Gaitley said. "I remember sitting with my players with 10,000 people going wild, and they're turning up the music and turning down the lights as their team is coming out of that tunnel. And then you hear, 'Back-to-back-to-back national champions.'

"We sort of looked at each other and go, 'Go, Hawks.' "

The Vols prevailed, 108-63.

Despite that humiliation, Gaitley is front and center when it comes to paying her respects to Summitt.

"Pat is a proven winner, she's classy, and she has the best interests of women's basketball and women at heart," Gaitley said. "You have to be in awe because you have so much respect for what she has accomplished. She is the only coach who has sustained what she built. She is always in the top 10, always in the NCAAs, always a national contender. A lot of other big schools can't do that. It's amazing. And it's because of Pat Summitt. She gets what she demands. She gets these kids who were all-everything in high school and gets them to do it her way."

Summitt's success and her place in the spotlight have not come without cost.

First, there is the pressure she puts on herself and her team to succeed. Her sideline fits — Summitt explodes from her chair over a disputed call by a referee or a bone-headed pass by one of her players — are legendary and almost frightening to watch. And her reputation as a perfectionist, taskmaster and unyielding disciplinarian is so widespread that many competing coaches use it to recruit against her. Of course, there is also jealousy.

Summitt long ago came to accept her reputation as an intense, driven workaholic because, well, it's true.

"It used to drive me crazy," she said. "Now I just accept it. That's who I am. All I can be is who I am. I can't be somebody else. I am not ashamed of who I am or my intensity."

Summit shrugged.

"I also have a reputation for being hard to play for," she added. "I don't think people who are goal-oriented and who are team players and hard workers have a hard time here. They love the intensity. They want to be on a winning team, and they love it here. If it was nothing but boot camp, how could we continue to recruit the best players in the country?"

Indeed, year after year, Summitt lures more than her share of the top prospects. The 1999-2000 season's four freshmen — guards April McDivitt and Kara Lawson, and forwards Tasheika Morris and Gwen Jackson — were all high school all-Americans.

The only two Tennesseeans on the team, sophomores Sara Edwards and Amanda Canon, were both high-school stars who turned down scholarship offers elsewhere to make the Vols as walk-ons.

If athletic skills are important for a Vol, so are the willingness and ability to fit into Summitt's unyielding system. First and foremost, you will turn yourself and your college career over to Summitt. She knows best. No matter how big a star you were in high school, you will accept the role she assigns you. You must buy into the concept of team over individual stardom. You must also be a hard worker, driven to succeed both on the court and in the classroom. Every Vol who has played under Summitt has eventually earned a degree.

"This program is not for everybody," Summitt said. "I want kids who have goals, who want to compete for national championships, who want a diploma, and who understand that going to class is not an option."

Even when players buy into all that, they arrive in Knoxville knowing that Summitt is going to yell at them and berate them and drive them harder than a rented mule.

A case in point was Kristen Clement, a junior point guard who had assumed the crucial role of on-court quarterback. Clement was a dominant, rapid-fire scorer and a three-time all-American at Cardinal O'Hara High School. Summitt had spotted her when she was 13 and playing in an AAU championship at the University of Tennessee. ("When I saw Ace, I said, 'If I have anything to do with it, I'm going to have a lefthanded point guard in a few years,'" Summitt recalls.)

Clement arrived in Knoxville and worked like a dog. She learned to hold her itchy trigger finger. She learned to play defense. She learned to think as quickly as she could whip the ball around the court. She still rode the bench and weathered her share of Summitt storms. Only moments after reaming out Snow, Summitt was barking at Clement.

"Somebody's always in the doghouse with Coach Summitt," Clement said after practice, smiling. "Point guards, it seems like every day. If anything goes wrong, it's your fault.

"But that is how she brings out the best in you. You cross that line, you better give 100 percent every day. She breaks you down to where you feel you can't play, you can't function in this program. But then she will build you back up. She really makes you a stronger woman from year to year, and she teaches you to take those values into life."

Do the players ever wave off a prospect they think won't cut it at Tennessee? "We're always straightforward," Clement said. "If you can't take the heat, this is not the place for you. If you want to be a national contender year in and year out, this is the place for you."

Ever regret coming here?

"No."

— *Joe Logan*

JERRY LODRIGUSS / Inquirer Staff Photographer

Oklahoma's Caton Hill (left) and UConn's Kelly Schumacher
followed the bouncing ball during their East Regional semifinal. The Huskies racked up a 102-80 victory.

Chapter 4

The Road to Philadelphia

*For the top 16 teams in the tournament — including
Penn State, Rutgers, Tennessee and Connecticut —
the road to Philly started in a familiar place: at home.
It was the reward for a successful regular season, and
although the buzz around the women's game is that
soon the NCAA will move the opening rounds to neu-
tral sites, the 2000 tournament began on campuses
across the country.*

Connecticut: An Overpowering Host

Welcome to the NCAA tournament's pro-am.

Each year, because the women's top 16 seeds open at
home, Connecticut gets placed in a foursome with three
awestruck amateurs on its home course.

Hampton, Clemson and Drake visited Storrs, Conn.,
when the NCAA tournament's East subregional teed off at
Gampel Pavilion. Connecticut was just working on its
swing. Anyone who thought the Huskies weren't going to
advance to the regionals in Richmond, Va., wasn't playing

with a full set of irons.

"It's a pleasure to be here," said Clemson coach Jim Davis, "although if I could have one choice of where to play, it wouldn't be Storrs."

In every season since 1994, Connecticut had played its first two NCAA games at Gampel. The Huskies were 12-0 in those contests with an average victory margin of 30 points. Overall, Connecticut had won 109 of its last 111 games in its on-campus arena.

And no one expected No. 16 seed Hampton, a 16-14 team that entered the Mid-Eastern Athletic Conference tourney with a losing record, to alter those trends.

As long as the top teams get the distinct edge of early-round home games, the women's tournament will remain slightly tainted. More March Foolishness than March Madness.

"I've always thought that [an all-neutral-site event] is what everybody wants," Geno Auriemma said. "And I'll be the first to say that that's what we have to do. I don't know when that will be a reality. There are a lot of factors that have to go into it. But sooner or later, it's got to happen.

"Sure, it's somewhat of an advantage to play your first two games on your home court. But 99 out of 100 times, in those early rounds, the better team is going to win anyway."

— *Frank Fitzpatrick*

And, true to form, the better teams did win. UConn flattened Hampton and then Clemson, despite worries from the Huskies coach. Before their tilt with the Tigers, Auriemma told his players: "You know what we're really good at? We're really good at crying on airplanes when we come back from the Final Eight."

*There would be no crying in Storrs. Nor in State
College, Pa., where Penn State beat Youngstown State
and Auburn to advance to the Sweet 16.*

For the Nittany Lions, a Major Step

Baby steps. Since finishing the 1996-97 season with a record of 15-12, Penn State had been taking baby steps in basketball. First, the Nittany Lions won the women's National Invitation Tournament in 1998. A year later, they advanced to the second round of the NCAA tournament before losing to Louisiana Tech.

Auburn was the "prove it" step. Prove you belong in the Sweet 16. Prove you have gotten better than a year ago. Prove you deserve to be mentioned in the same breath as Final Four and Philadelphia.

Prove it Penn State did, staving off a pesky Auburn team, 75-69, to advance to the Midwest Regional semifinals in Kansas City, Mo. It marked the program's first trip to the Sweet 16 since the 1996 tournament, and coach Rene Portland's eighth in 20 years at Penn State.

"We're thrilled," Portland said afterward. "This really shows the growth and what these kids have been able to do for Lady Lions basketball, to go from nothing to the NIT champions to the second round last year. Now we're the second seed and host of a regional. That's what they're supposed to do, protect the [Bryce] Jordan Center."

When the final buzzer sounded, Chrissy Falcone jumped into Maren Walseth's arms, and the team convened in a circle at midcourt. Andrea Garner, who tied a career high with 14 rebounds, breathed a sigh of relief. Her family from Philadelphia had already bought tickets to Kansas City.

VICKI VALERIO / Inquirer Staff Photographer

Penn State's Andrea Garner grabbed a rebound in front of
Auburn's Kris Bernath during their second-round NCAA game
in State College, Pa. The Lions roared to a 75-69 win.

"Today was a great day for us," Garner said after the game. "Everyone knew going in that today was either the day we showed it or we didn't show it. And we showed it."

"Their eyes are on the prize," Portland said. "There's an empty trophy stand. There's a picture of the Liberty Bell. We got them postcards to send from Kansas City the other day so they can send them out to people. But their eye is on the prize, and don't ever doubt that."

— *Ashley McGeachy*

Tennessee, historically dominant in Knoxville, cruised into the Sweet 16 with wins over Furman and Arizona. Only Rutgers had any sense of intrigue. The Scarlet Knights beat Holy Cross in the opening round, then had to deal with the sentimental favorite, St. Joseph's, which was hoping to have a home-court advantage at the Final Four. Rutgers had another idea.

Rutgers Finishes Off St. Joe's

The Rutgers women kept their mission on the mark in Piscataway, N.J., by snuffing out the St. Joseph's Hawks' dream of becoming Cinderella at the Final Four in Philadelphia. The second-seeded Scarlet Knights allowed the 10th-seeded Hawks few wisps of offense in a 59-39 triumph in a West subregional game at Rutgers' Louis Brown Athletic Center.

It was the Hawks' lowest point production since a 66-33 shutdown by Cheyney State in February 1983. The coach on the bench opposite St. Joseph's in that contest was the same as the one on Rutgers' bench — Vivian Stringer.

While a Sweet 16 appearance remained out of reach for

St. Joseph's, Rutgers returned for a third straight season.

"We weren't going to be intimidated. We weren't going to back down," St. Joseph's coach Stephanie Gaitley said. "But to be honest, they have better players."

The Hawks limited Rutgers star Shawnetta Stewart to 1-for-10 shooting and just two points, but the rest of Stringer's group made up the difference.

"Anytime you look at the statistics and say, 'All right, you held their leading scorer to two points, you forced the team to shoot 36 percent, and have 17 offensive rebounds,' you have to be there at the end," Gaitley said. "But the game came down to their role players stepping up. That was huge. [Point guard] Tasha Pointer did a super job. Usha Gilmore hit some big shots when they needed them."

Gaitley remained upbeat afterward.

"I told the players in the locker room to enjoy what they did," she said. "They took St. Joe's to another step on the national scene. I can honestly say I feel my players gave their all. When you can walk away feeling like a winner, regardless of the score, and feeling like you did things the right way, then you can walk to the Final Four feeling good about yourself."

— *Mel Greenberg*

The second week of the tournament held a few more surprises. Tennessee had the shortest trip — a cross-state trek to Memphis' Pyramid, which was filled with orange-clad supporters for their Mideast Regional semifinal against Virginia. The opponent was a familiar one for Pat Summitt, who seemingly always must get through the Cavaliers to advance in the tournament.

Loss to Virginia in '90 Haunts Tennessee

Planning or arrogance?

In 1990, Tennessee couldn't be faulted for either. The Volunteers were the reigning national champions and the favorites to repeat. Plus, they were slated to host the Final Four in Thompson-Boling Arena, where they had lost just one game — to Louisiana Tech by a single point — all season.

So before securing a spot in the Final Four, the Vols had T-shirts made declaring, "Three and Tennessee," in the Final Four. It would have been a catchy phrase, if not for Dawn Staley and Virginia, who instead dictated that the slogan read, "Three and an Upstart."

On a surreal Saturday in Norfolk, Va., Staley and the underdog Cavaliers dealt Pat Summitt what she described as "the toughest loss of my career," a 79-75 overtime shocker in the East Regional title game that prevented the Vols from reigning supreme at home. In 11 meetings between the schools, it had been Virginia's only victory, a fact the Atlantic Coast Conference regular-season champion again tried to change when it faced top-seeded Tennessee at the Pyramid.

"Tennessee is a very formidable opponent," said Virginia coach Debbie Ryan. "They have great athleticism. They are an excellent team. We are a team that is a little bit of a surprise this year, but I don't think that we are looking at this as just being glad to be here."

The Cavaliers were happy to be in Norfolk in '90, after which they sent a frazzled Summitt home to deal with disappointed fans. But Virginia, still on a high from the win, lost to Stanford in the semifinal, a game that is one of

VICKI VALERIO / Inquirer Staff Photographer

Tennessee's Tamika Catchings deposited a layup against
Texas Tech's Plenette Pierson. The Vols vanquished the
Raiders, 57-44, in the Mideast Regional final in Memphis, Tenn.

Ryan's biggest disappointments. "I don't know if I ever came off that [Tennessee] high," she said.

Tennessee, however, regrouped from the low. Summitt made the 1990-91 Vols wear those "Three and Tennessee" T-shirts as practice gear. They had orange shorts, blue shorts, black shorts and white shorts, but the T-shirts never changed.

"That was our motivation," said Nikki Caldwell, a freshman on that Tennessee team who became an assistant at Virginia.

And it worked, as the Vols got revenge, coming back from 17 down against Virginia to win the 1991 regional title by 70-67, again in overtime.

The rivalry between Tennessee and Virginia hadn't been lost on any of the current players, but the Vols' Kara Lawson, a self-described "UVA kid at heart," probably had felt the Cavaliers' pain more than most.

"I always remember that the University of Virginia would get so far, and this one team would come and always beat them, and that team was Tennessee," said Lawson, who grew up in Springfield, Va. "I never liked it."

— *Ashley McGeachy*

But Lawson didn't mind this game. The UVA kid wore orange and white, and a victorious smile afterward.

Tennessee Waltzes Past Cavaliers

For 26 seasons, Pat Summitt had tried to field a team that would play with rugged intensity and reckless abandon for 40 minutes, not for just a few. Try as she might, she had never succeeded, not even in 1998, when she led the "best team I've ever coached" to a third consecutive NCAA title.

But, to borrow from Nolan Richardson, 40 minutes of hell has never been a prerequisite for Tennessee to win, and it wasn't against Virginia. Thirty minutes of an orange-and-white attack was sufficient to send the Cavaliers home losers. Thirty minutes of Tamika Catchings' brilliance, the Volunteers' dogged defensive pressure, and dominance on the offensive glass led to Tennessee's 31st win of the season, 77-56.

The victory propelled the Vols into the Mideast Regional final against Texas Tech, a 68-65 winner over Notre Dame.

Tennessee threatened to blow the game open in the first 10 minutes. Catchings, the Naismith player of the year, scored the opening six points of the game, and the Vols raced to a 17-5 lead. Virginia's first basket came after four turnovers and three missed field goals, and by the time the Cavaliers had scored 11 points, they also had made 11 turnovers and trailed by 15.

"The first 5 1/2 minutes were a nightmare," Virginia coach Debbie Ryan said after her team finished the season 25-9. "I knew that was going to be the case, but I felt like we were very prepared. I felt like we'd be able to run the floor."

— *Ashley McGeachy*

Meanwhile, Penn State was in the center of steakhouses, barbecue and jazz — Kansas City, Mo. The Lions were two games away from the promised land, and coach Rene Portland's first Final Four.

Penn State's Magic Number: Two

This represented quite a detour when traveling between State College, Pa., and Philadelphia, but it marked the last stop for the Penn State Nittany Lions on the road to their coveted goal of reaching the NCAA women's Final Four. But the Lions knew they had to be focused on two more wins.

"If I don't put it out of my mind," Portland said, "somebody will. I think we've done a very good job of dividing our season into different periods of what we wanted to do goal-wise. You have to keep your eye on the prize, but I think they've done a terrific job in regrouping after losses and being mature about the whole thing."

Andrea Garner, who had averaged 14.8 points, 8.7 rebounds and 2.3 blocked shots per game, understood the perils of dreaming about finishing her collegiate career in Philadelphia, but she admitted the thought was there.

"At this time, you really can't look too far ahead," she said. "Every team presents a big challenge for us. There's no way I can look too far in advance, but it's definitely in the back of my mind. It's a goal, and it's there. I'm on the court knowing that my family and friends are waiting to see me there."

— *Joe Juliano*

Penn State defeated Iowa State, 66-65, while Connecticut, playing in Richmond, dealt with Oklahoma after a few nervous minutes.

After Slow Start, Huskies Breeze

Connecticut trailed by 9-8 (that is not a typographical error). In some of the tonier Hartford suburbs, stunned Huskies fans no doubt were driving their BMWs into trees. Geno Auriemma pivoted on his Italian loafers and signaled toward his bench. Asjha Jones and Tamika Williams popped up, tore off their sweats, and sprinted toward the

JERRY LODRIGUSS / Inquirer Staff Photographer

The Huskies' Svetlana Abrosimova (25) pursued the ball with Oklahoma's LaNeishea Caufield in the East Regional semifinal in Richmond, Va.

scorer's table. Within minutes, a familiar calm had returned to Connecticut.

Jones immediately hit two spinning shots in the lane. Williams added a third basket. And Connecticut was off on an 18-0 run that ended what little suspense there was in a 102-80 victory over Oklahoma in an NCAA tournament East Regional semifinal at the Alltel Pavilion in Richmond, Va.

Jones and Williams each finished with a team-high 16 points as the all-American-laden Connecticut bench wore out one more opponent on their cruise-control journey to the Final Four. The Huskies won their first three NCAA games by a total of 131 points.

"What concerns you is their hunger, their desire," Oklahoma coach Sherri Coale said. "They know where they want to go and how to get there."

Having gotten to a regional final for the third time in four years, the Huskies were one victory away from a Final Four that would reunite the perpetually hungry Auriemma with the Philadelphia delicacies he craves.

"There's a big difference between getting to a Final Four and winning a national championship," he said. "I keep telling these kids that a lot of teams get to Final Fours but only a special few win national championships."

Connecticut got nearly as many points from its reserves (47) as its starters.

"They come at you in waves," said Coale. "They never worry about fouls. If one girl gets in foul trouble, they take her out and bring someone else in. They don't give you a chance to breathe. I don't know of any team that can come at you with that many great players."

Jones, Williams and freshman point guard Kennitra Johnson sank the scrappy Sooners (25-8) during that first-half burst. The reserves were fresh and quick, and they picked off pass after pass from the wearying Oklahoma starters — of the Sooners' 33 turnovers, 21 were from steals.

"Our bench is just awesome," said Connecticut's Shea Ralph, who finished with 10 points, eight assists and five steals. "Our starters are solid, but we have five or six players on our bench who could start as well. Lots of times we're even better with them in there. ... Asjha might be the most talented player on our team."

Connecticut had beaten Oklahoma by 16 points in Norman earlier in the season. Coale didn't see much difference in the Huskies a few months later.

"They are used to being in the regionals," she said. "This was like another conference game for them. We're like a kid in a candy store. They live here."

— *Frank Fitzpatrick*

Meanwhile, Rutgers, which had to travel across three time zones to Portland, Ore., dispatched Alabama-Birmingham.

Rutgers Gets Closer to the Big Dance

Vivian Stringer's second-seeded Rutgers squad finished off the Cinderella run of 11th-seeded Alabama-Birmingham, 60-45 in a West Regional semifinal in front of 6,914 at Memorial Coliseum.

The triumph elevated Rutgers to the Elite Eight for the second consecutive season.

To advance to the Final Four, the Scarlet Knights would have to find a way past talented and top-seeded Georgia, which pulverized fifth-seeded North Carolina, 83-57.

To get the job done against UAB, Rutgers relied on its tenacious defense. And it found enough punch to stay just out of the reach of the Blazers. This was especially true in the five minutes of the second half, when UAB closed its deficit to 34-32 with 15:03 to play.

Mia Thrash scored the Blazers' first seven points in that run to bring her team close. Rutgers, meanwhile, suffered through a drought of 7:41 at the end of the first half and the beginning of the second in which it managed just two points.

Rutgers never trailed in the first half and jumped on the scoreboard, 3-0, on a three-pointer by junior point guard Tasha Pointer two minutes into the game.

A steal by Davalyn Cunningham followed by two foul shots by Karlita Washington made it 5-0 with 17:16 remaining in the half. Then UAB center Michelle Smith scored her team's first two points off an assist from Holly Holland. The Scarlet Knights built their lead to 32-23 by halftime.

— Mel Greenberg

The last Monday in March was a made-for-ESPN night, with three games on the flagship station while Penn State-Louisiana Tech was televised nationally on the deuce, ESPN2. Penn State's Rene Portland knew the Nittany Lions' game with Louisiana Tech could elevate her to the highest coaching status.

Portland Can See the Promised Land

Rene Portland is aware of how modern society measures the success of a coach or player. She followed the retirement of Dan Marino and heard the talk about his never winning a Super Bowl. She read what was said about Gene Keady's not being able to reach a men's NCAA Final Four with Purdue.

In Kansas City, Mo., Portland prepared to lead Penn State to its first NCAA women's Final Four, a crowning achievement to a marvelous career in which she had won 465 games in 20 seasons as the Nittany Lions' coach. For Portland, it was a chance to make history and realize a dream of playing for the national championship in her home area of Philadelphia.

She wanted to do this for her players and her school, however, not for those who gauge the success of an accomplished program solely by the number of Final Four appearances.

"Penn State has been there all the time; it really has," Portland said. "But when you listen to ESPN say, 'They're the only program in the top 10 that has not made it,' it seems like everybody's searching for something. You just shake your head. There is respect for the program. We know we can recruit nationally, and we've done that.

"But it would mean a lot [to reach a Final Four] and get the monkey off of our back, to be quite honest. The bottom line is that it comes down to the players. This is the last hurrah for our seniors; I'll be able to come back and keep fighting this war. But it will be neat to see them leave another stamp on Lady Lion basketball."

"It would mean a lot to the program, and it would mean a lot to Coach," center Andrea Garner said. "To get to Philadelphia would mean a lot to all of us who are from there. It would put the program beyond a point it's ever reached before. It's something the seniors would definitely take pride in."

Louisiana Tech, which eliminated Old Dominion, 86-74, in the semifinal, also had some extra motivation, though it had been to 13 Final Fours and won three national championships. Techsters coach Leon Barmore had announced he would retire after the season. (In April, he changed his mind and decided to return.)

Barmore, who declined to answer questions about his retirement before the game, was more than willing to talk of Portland's quest for her first Final Four.

"The lady's a good coach, and it's been that way for years," he said. "It does start to gnaw on you, I'm sure in her case, because in our society it's the Final Four; it's probably [emphasized] too much. But I think that someday it will happen."

He paused, then added: "Heaven forbid."

— *Joe Juliano*

That day was closer than Barmore would have liked.

Penn State Marches Into Final Four

Andrea Garner didn't walk off the court at Municipal Auditorium. She floated, wearing a smile much bigger than her 6 feet, 3 inches of height. The Penn State center was going home to Philadelphia to play for a national championship.

Garner, Helen Darling, Lisa Shepherd and the rest of the Penn State Nittany Lions played a near-flawless first half in the NCAA Midwest Regional final against Louisiana Tech, and cruised to an 86-65 pasting of the Techsters and a trip to the school's first NCAA women's Final Four.

With Shepherd accounting for 20 first-half points, the Lions (30-4) roared out to a 45-29 halftime lead against the Techsters (31-3). Penn State never allowed its opponent to get closer than 15 points in the entire second half.

Garner was removed from the game with 1 minute, 27 seconds to play after scoring 15 points and grabbing 12 rebounds. She skipped to the sideline and received multiple hugs from Portland and her teammates.

"We've been talking about it and talking about it since the beginning of the year, since last year," Garner said. "I'm speechless right now. All I can say is, I'm going home. We said from the beginning we were going back there. We had a lot of people behind us and we appreciate everybody's support."

Then there was Shepherd, who accounted for only two

points in the semifinal win over Iowa State. With Penn State trailing, 20-19, at the 12-minute mark of the first half, she nailed a 16-foot jumper to touch off an 18-4 run that gave the Lions control of the game.

Shepherd hit 5 of 6 shots — including three consecutive three-point attempts — for 13 points during that eight-minute stretch. She hit the final basket of the spurt, a three-pointer with 3:40 to play, to give the Nittany Lions a 37-24 lead.

"I felt from the very beginning that this was our night," said Shepherd, who finished with a game-high 25 points, including 4 of 6 from behind the arc, plus nine rebounds. "I think we all came in with that attitude. We believe in each other and we knew we could get it done."

"Our execution in the first half was just perfection," said Portland, who was raised in Broomall and was part of Immaculata's three national championship teams. "If we can get four more [halves] like that in a row, then we'll be wearing a different kind of [championship] hat. But tonight was fun. They did what they had to do — rebound, hustle and believe in themselves."

— *Joe Juliano*

Connecticut's Auriemma had to direct his Huskies into the Final Four to secure an all-Philadelphia-coached semifinal. He would not be denied.

UConn Punches Its Ticket to Philly

There were times in this game, as he tried to push visions of Villanova-Georgetown out of his head, when it looked as if Geno Auriemma's next cheesesteak was going to come at some Connecticut mall. The Connecticut coach's homecoming, and his No.1-ranked team's expected

JERR Y LODRIGUSS / Inquirer Staff Photographer

Shea Ralph embraced coach Geno Auriemma as the Huskies put the finishing touches on an 86-71 win over Louisiana State in the East Regional final. The Tigers had thrown a scare into UConn.

coronation at the Final Four in Philadelphia, barely survived a rainy night in Richmond, Va.

Louisiana State, poised and gutsy and having played a near-perfect first half, hung with the top-seeded Huskies for most of the NCAA tournament's East Regional final at Alltel Pavilion. But the Huskies' pressure and remarkable depth drained third-seeded LSU, and Connecticut held on, 86-71.

"I'd been thinking about Villanova-Georgetown in '85 as the game went on, and [Villanova] didn't shoot 74 percent in the first half," said Auriemma. "I couldn't believe it."

With the victory, the Huskies advanced to their fourth Final Four in a decade, their first since 1996.

"I think in the last minute, it finally hit us," said Shea Ralph, the feisty Connecticut all-American who had 13 points. "That's when we realized that we were going to the Final Four at last."

The Huskies' players formed a noisy mass at center court as soon as the buzzer sounded. They stayed right there, donning Final Four shirts and caps and squealing with delight every few seconds.

"It's really nice for these girls," said Auriemma. "You know, sometimes in practice when I ask them to do something hard, they don't understand. But I do it because I know there are going to be times like this, times when they are tested. That's why you do it."

It was the Huskies' first real challenge since a 49-45 win at Rutgers on Feb. 12.

"You'd have to say Connecticut is the favorite," LSU coach Sue Gunter said of the Final Four. "They've been No. 1 all year, and they went 1-1 with Tennessee."

"I tell them that scoring a lot of points doesn't mean a thing," Auriemma said. "But getting to the Final Four,

that's something they'll look back on 30 years from now
and say, 'You know what? That was quite an accomplishment.' "

— *Frank Fitzpatrick*

*Then Tennessee rolled into yet another Final Four, Pat
Summitt's 12th after a one-year hiatus.*

After a Scare, Vols Join the Party

First Kenyon Martin. Then Tamika Catchings. The
Pyramid in Memphis hadn't been kind to the Naismith
players of the year in March.

But unlike the Cincinnati men's team, which lost to
Saint Louis in the Conference USA tournament after its
superstar broke his leg, the Tennessee women withstood
an unsettling injury to their top star to win their 32d game
of the season.

Popular opinion had Cincinnati, pre-Martin injury,
advancing to the Final Four of the men's NCAA tournament. By beating Texas Tech, 57-44, the Vols did what the
Bearcats couldn't — meet expectations. After a one-year
hiatus from the Final Four, Tennessee earned a trip to
Philadelphia.

But the Vols didn't win without distress. Late in the
second half, playing on a wobbly, sprained right ankle,
Catchings struggled offensively. She would penetrate but
then charge into her defender or she would get smothered
and miss altogether.

However, with Tennessee up by only 44-42, she turned
on other areas of her game. She aggressively went for a
defensive rebound, battled Raiders forward Aleah
Johnson to the floor and drew the foul, making both free

VICKI VALERIO / Inquirer Staff Photographer

Keitha Dickerson of Texas Tech couldn't keep Tennessee's
Tamika Catchings from this rebound in the Mideast Regional
final. Catchings suffered a sprained right ankle in the game,
but the Vols prevailed.

throws for a 46-42 lead. After trading possessions, Catchings drew a charge on Johnson and then watched when Semeka Randall scored for a 48-42 lead.

At the other end, Amber Tarr launched a three-point shot only to have Catchings swat it, grab the ball and feed April McDivitt, who found Michelle Snow for a layup and a 50-52 lead. That was all the Vols would need to secure a spot in their fourth women's Final Four in five years.

"We tried to keep her from scoring, and we didn't do that good of a job keeping her off [the boards]," Johnson said. "There were times when we thought we had her blocked out, but that's the way the ball bounces."

With 10:47 remaining in the first half and Tennessee leading, 12-10, Catchings missed a foul-line jumper, and her right foot landed on Tarr's foot. Catchings' ankle twisted under her weight, and she collapsed in a moaning heap on the floor, less than two feet from where Martin went down.

With Tennessee's trainer holding her right leg, Catchings audibly sobbed for several minutes, finally sat up, and was virtually carried off the court.

"My foot rolled over, and it felt like it snapped," Catchings said. "That's the first time I've ever sprained my ankle on that side, and the first time's always a killer. ... It hurt when I came back out, but I wanted to be out there for my teammates."

— *Ashley McGeachy*

Finally, in a game televised at midnight on the East Coast, Rutgers became the third team Vivian Stringer had led to the Final Four. Before the game, Stringer said the Scarlet Knights would "have to bring an 'A' game, or we'll be history." They played well enough.

Rutgers Earns a Homecoming for Stringer

Rutgers' season-long dream became a reality in the West Regional final in Portland, Ore., when the second-seeded Scarlet Knights upset top-seeded Georgia, 59-51, to advance to the First Union Center and the national semifinals.

It marked the first NCAA women's Final Four appearance for Rutgers (26-7), which won the last championship of the Association for Intercollegiate Athletics for Women by beating Texas at the Palestra in Philadelphia in 1982. The triumph was especially sweet for Rutgers coach Vivian Stringer, who, also in 1982, guided Cheyney State to the first NCAA title game, where it lost to Louisiana Tech.

By winning, Stringer extended a record by taking a third program to the women's Final Four. In 1993, she guided Iowa to a semifinal appearance before it lost to Ohio State.

The defeat was a tough one for Georgia (32-4), which many believed had the talent to grab a national title. The Bulldogs, who were a solid preseason bet to get to Philadelphia, overran Southeastern Conference rival Tennessee, 78-51, in January at home in Athens.

— *Mel Greenberg*

Chapter 5

The Arrival of the Philly Four

The turnaround from the regional finals to the Final Four is extraordinarily quick. No sooner did Tennessee get back to Knoxville than it was off again. Kristen Clement had time for a few loads of laundry, while Tamika Catchings hung out with her boyfriend, a starter on the Tennessee men's team. Geno Auriemma brought his Huskies in on Tuesday, while Rutgers had charter problems out of Oregon and didn't arrive in Philadelphia until Wednesday afternoon. The only consolation was that Temple coach John Chaney, a longtime friend of Vivian Stringer's, was waiting, a bouquet of flowers in his arms.

A Philadelphia Accent for the Final Four

Whoever said you can't go home again obviously didn't understand what a powerful draw a Division I women's Final Four in Philadelphia proved to be for some of the

ERIC MENCHER / Inquirer Staff Photographer

Penn State's arrival for the Final Four drew a crowd of enthusiastic followers to the Lions' hotel in Center City. Basketball players from Our Lady of Calvary School in Northeast Philadelphia greeted the bus.

most prestigious graduates of the city game.

This NCAA tournament may have been the biggest big-city extravaganza yet in the women's game when it unfolded at the First Union Center.

Still, the big stage did not camouflage the cozy feel of a family reunion, thanks to all the local legends who returned as coaches and players for the national championship round.

You can't get much more local resonance than that of a possible championship game between the state universities of Pennsylvania and New Jersey. All Penn State and Rutgers had to do to keep the title very much in the family was to defeat the top two teams in the land.

This was quixotic, perhaps, but no more so than the year-long dream of happy homecomings finally realized by the three coaches with strong Philadelphia ties (Vivian Stringer of Rutgers, Rene Portland of Penn State, and Geno Auriemma of Connecticut), and by four players (Shawnetta Stewart of Rutgers, Kristen Clement of Tennessee, and Andrea Garner and Rashana Barnes of Penn State).

Rutgers, ranked eighth in the nation, got the first shot at completing the dream when Stringer's Knights played Pat Summitt's mighty Tennessee Vols in the opener of the national semifinal round.

Stringer, who made her name as a coach at Cheyney State, had combined with Summitt for more than 1,300 Division I coaching victories, making this a classic battle between two pioneers of the modern women's game.

Penn State took on UConn in the second semifinal, as Broomall's Portland faced Norristown's Auriemma in another chess match between two venerable coaches.

Just the presence of Stringer, Portland and Auriemma assured this Final Four of its most poignant Philadelphia angles.

Stringer helped write NCAA history when she took tiny Cheyney State out of the Philadelphia suburbs and into national prominence in the inaugural NCAA tournament in 1982.

Now Stringer was back, and in record fashion. With

more than 600 coaching victories, she became the first coach in Division I basketball — men's or women's — to take three schools to the Final Four. Stringer's Iowa team played in the Final Four 11 years after the '82 Cheyney team lost the title game to Louisiana Tech.

Temple's John Chaney had been Stringer's friend and mentor dating to their days at Cheyney when they made the men's and women's teams national powers.

Chaney may have missed out on another chance at his first Final Four in 2000, but a hybrid form of his matchup defense, as designed by Stringer, was in the women's version.

Rutgers' puzzling zone had stifled all comers in the NCAA tournament, even Georgia, the top seed in the West, by 59-51. The Knights also won because of an equally impressive offensive effort by Shawnetta Stewart. She scored 22 points to assure that her collegiate career would end where her high school career did, right back in Philly.

The Knights' victory came after Penn State became the first No. 2 seed to dispatch the region's best this year. The Nittany Lions upset Louisiana Tech, 86-65, in the Midwest, enabling Portland, like Stringer, to come full circle. Portland, of Broomall, was in her first Final Four as a coach after 24 years of trying.

"She's been in there I don't know how long — longer than I am old," said Andrea Garner, who scored 15 points and pocketed 12 rebounds against the school commonly known as La Tech. "She writes on the board, 'This is our time.' It's her time, too."

The clock nearly struck for the Lions, though, in the regional semifinals against Iowa State. Garner quickly fell into foul trouble, and Penn State fell behind. That's when Barnes, another athletic low-post player, came in and held

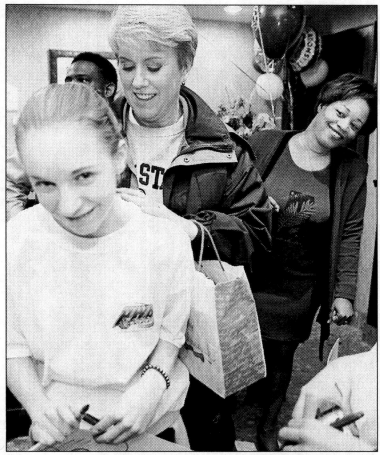

ERIC MENCHER / Inquirer Staff Photographer

Penn State coach Rene Portland autographed the T-shirt of a young fan, Kris Aquilino, as the Lions arrived for the national semifinals.

the fort until her team could rally for a one-point win.

"I'm happy for Rene Portland," Auriemma said, "because she's worked a long time to get to the Final Four. She's had some great teams in the past and it's never happened for her. She played at Immaculata, grew up in the area, has lots of family there."

Ah, but doesn't everyone?

Even though the legendary Summitt is all Tennessee, her Vols still fit well within the Philly family guidelines, what with the presence of Clement, a guard out of Cardinal O'Hara High.

And let's not forget Tamika Catchings. The national player of the year, who delivered the Vols to an easy 57-44 victory over Texas Tech in the Mideast Regional despite severely spraining her ankle, is the daughter of Harvey Catchings, who played in the NBA for — who else? — the 76ers.

Then there's Auriemma, as Philadelphia as a cheese-steak.

That history and those ties made Auriemma's fourth Final Four in nine years and first since 1996 all the more special.

"I'm happy for my mom; she'll get a chance to see this," said Auriemma, his voice cracking as the consequence of a surprisingly tense 86-71 victory over Louisiana State in the East Regional final finally registered.

He said that during the stress of the game, "I kept thinking about growing up — every time somebody asked me to do something, I always tried to do it. I always felt responsible from the time I was a kid. And I felt a tremendous sense of responsibility to get these kids to a Final Four."

He did, bringing UConn to the basketball breeding ground he loves, an accomplishment only Portland, Stringer and the Philly kids will ever fully understand.

— *Claire Smith*

For PWB 2000, Final Four week culminated a lengthy fund-raising and planning drive. Now was their time for the organizers to show off the work, and they started with an announcement that, yes, they had reached their fund-raising goal.

For the Fund-Raisers, a Victory

Two days before the Final Four, Philadelphia Women's Basketball 2000 officials announced that they had exceeded their yearlong fund-raising goal to support activities during the NCAA women's Final Four.

"PWB 2000 has met its fund-raising goals of $1.4 million," said G. Fred DiBona Jr., cochairman of the organizing committee for championship week, at a news conference at the Pennsylvania Convention Center. "In fact, with Rosemarie [Grieco], Cathy [Andruzzi] and others, no one should be surprised we exceeded that goal."

DiBona thanked the corporate community, adding, "The call was answered with great enthusiasm, and we're so very proud of our corporations throughout the region to make this possible."

A month earlier, PWB 2000 was still $500,000 short, but in subsequent weeks the state and city each met the organizers' requests for financial grants. Contributions also were received from Comcast-Spectacor, the sports and entertainment entity that owns the First Union Center, and Aramark, which runs food and support services.

Andruzzi praised the media's attention to activities surrounding the women's Final Four as well as the teams themselves. "It's been unbelievable," she said. "That's a tribute to the city of Philadelphia. That's a tribute to women's basketball. That's a tribute to how big the sport really is."

Added Grieco: "About a year ago, we sort of held hands

and pushed forward — and sometimes we had to pull along the way — to reach this goal. Today we're here to hold hands again, but this time in applause."

— *Mel Greenberg*

For Auriemma, the Final Four culminated a year-long trek back home, where he could introduce his players to cheesesteaks and host a party for a couple hundred of his closest friends.

Auriemma Revels in His Return Home

Geno Auriemma watched his Connecticut players interact with the noisy crowd that had gathered to meet them at Philadelphia International Airport. He laughed as they strained to understand the heavily accented auto- graph requests and greetings.

"Yo, welcome to Fluff-ya! We luv youse gurls!"

"I think they were amazed to see that there are other people who talk like me," said Auriemma, who had retained his accent and his Philly swagger while building one of the nation's top women's programs in distinctly nonurban Storrs, Conn.

Despite the nonstop phone calls and ticket requests, Connecticut's coach was cherishing this women's Final Four homecoming. If there was any free time, he had enough plans to fill a week and several stomachs.

Before he even had checked into the Sheraton Society Hill, he was talking with lip-smacking relish about his wish list, most of which he would abandon in the flurry of team dinners and award ceremonies, practices and news con- ferences.

He hoped to hit some South Philly restaurants and

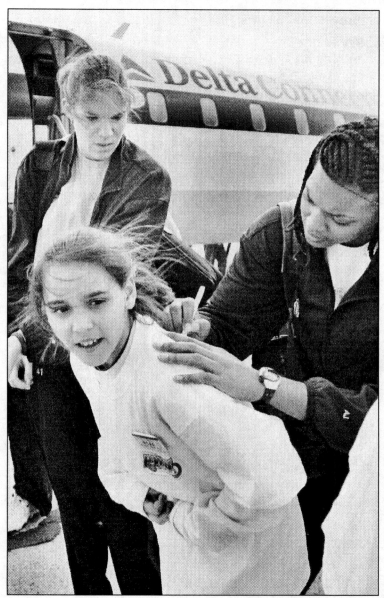

JOHN COSTELLO / Inquirer Staff Photographer

Connecticut's Paige Sauer (left) and Asjha Jones provided
autographs for a happy fan, Dana Baiocco, after the Huskies
touched down at Philadelphia International Airport.

sandwich shops, visit his cousin's Italian Market shop, sample his mother's home cooking, maybe take his kids on a sentimental journey to Norristown, where he might want to reacquaint himself with his favorite sandwich shop.

There's a brother in Norristown, a sister near there, and old Bishop Kenrick pals like Tommy Grady and Paul McDade. Then there's his best buddy, St. Joseph's University men's basketball coach Phil Martelli.

"You can just see it in his face, how happy he is to be back here," Martelli said. "One of the secretaries in our office saw him on the news and she said, 'He seems real cocky.' And I told her that no, he's just got that sarcasm we all have in Philly. It's not meant to hurt anyone. Geno would give you the shirt off his back. And I know he is just really, really excited about being in Philly."

Auriemma wanted to get to South Philly, where a cousin owns Claudio's King of Cheese on South Ninth Street. He wanted to stop by Cheesesteak Row on Passyunk Avenue, a site as sacred to the UConn coach as the Women's Basketball Hall of Fame.

"Last time we were in town, I took the team down there," Auriemma said. "Half of them ate at Geno's, half at Pat's. Me, I stayed in the middle of the street and had some of both. I wasn't going to pick one over the other."

Perpetually hungry, Auriemma planned to travel to Phoenixville for some of his widowed mother's pasta and gravy. And from there he thought about taking his three children — two teenage girls and a son in fifth grade — back to the old neighborhood.

"There's really not much for me in Norristown now," he said. "My dad passed away a few years ago. My mom lives near my sister out by Phoenixville. But maybe I'll bring the kids there so they can see where the real people live. So they know it's not all this [gesturing toward surrounding Society Hill] and Connecticut."

Martelli, who hired Auriemma as his assistant when he coached the Bishop Kenrick boys' basketball team two decades ago, can't look at Auriemma without thinking of those days.

"Neither of us are big drinkers, but after every Friday game, we'd go to the Glass Rack [a defunct Norristown bar] and talk basketball," Martelli said. "After a few beers and a lot of talk, we could turn 20-point losses into five-point wins as quick as you could eat a cheesesteak. We never lost a game there."

When they weren't talking basketball, they were discussing the Phillies and Eagles.

"Sports, sports, sports," Martelli said. "Geno had a party at his apartment when the Eagles were in the Super Bowl. I had one when the Phillies were in the World Series."

Auriemma read The Inquirer, Daily News and Norristown Times Herald every day, a habit that has made him extremely accommodating to the pack of writers that accompany his No. 1 team everywhere.

"He understands what we need," said John Altavilla of the Hartford Courant.

After the basketball season ended, Martelli and Auriemma would meet every afternoon at 5 at Center Square Golf Course.

"We didn't have two dimes to rub together, so we would sneak into golf courses whenever we could. But at Center Square you could play for $5 after 5 p.m.," Martelli recalled. "I never got any good at the game, but Geno did.

"We'd play till it got dark. When we were finished, we'd grab a couple of sandwiches at Lou's on Main Street or at this place called the Meadowbrook and take them back home. Then we'd talk about basketball some more. It was basketball 365 days a year."

As the two men grew older, their interests widened. Auriemma, said Martelli, began to read more, mostly biographies, and developed an interest in music and wine.

"But don't be fooled," Martelli said. "He's still a Philly guy."

— *Frank Fitzpatrick*

Tennessee's Ace Clement, with her stylish attire and glamour-girl looks, also was Philly through and through. The icon from Cardinal O'Hara High struggled throughout the season, but she hoped a homecoming would break her out of her slump.

The Glamour Girl: Kristen Clement

She is an unapologetic glamour girl who has won three beauty pageants, describes her fashion style as "elegant," and, unlike her Tennessee teammates, curls her hair and wears makeup when she plays. Even so, Kristen Clement has enough tomboy in her — and enough game, too — that those who know her best call her "Ace" and have been calling her Ace since she was embarrassing boys on the playgrounds of Broomall.

The ace of hearts triumphantly returned to Philadelphia for the Final Four.

"Playing for a national championship in your hometown ... it brings a different level and different emotions," the junior guard said before the big weekend while doing laundry in her apartment in Knoxville, Tenn. "I'm very excited."

ERIC MENCHER / Inquirer Staff Photographer

Kristen Clement performed a juggling act at practice as the Vols tuned up for the national semifinals at the First Union Center. Her Philadelphia homecoming would take an unfortunate twist at a practice three days later.

A lifetime had passed since the legend left Cardinal O'Hara High, bound for the Tennessee mountains. As a prep phenom, Clement led Cardinal O'Hara to three Catholic League titles and, in her senior year, to a 27-1 record and No. 8 national ranking. She was a scoring machine, piling up 2,256 points, a feat that prompted Cardinal O'Hara to hang her No. 33 jersey alongside Illinois coach Theresa Grentz's No. 12.

Clement's following in Philly was almost cultish. But her new teammates in Knoxville weren't used to a confident 18-year-old in form-fitting clothes and platform heels.

"There are very different types of basketball players, just like there are different people who like to do different things," said Clement's classmate Tamika Catchings of Duncanville, Texas. "Some people think makeup doesn't have a place in basketball. But as long as you perform, I guess it's OK."

Catchings wears lip balm and a blue headband to keep her hair off her face. Clement, who averaged 5.6 points and 3.1 rebounds and had a team high of 122 assists, sports lipstick, sparkly pink eye shadow, eyeliner and mascara, all tastefully applied and amazingly resistant to sweat.

But she said her proclivity to makeup wasn't based on vanity. Female athletes, she said, can be glamorous, too.

"That's what I'm trying to portray," Clement said. "Growing up and watching females, they didn't look like females. They had that athletic, manly look, but they didn't look like women. I was like, 'I just want to let people know girls can be girls and be mean.' It's OK to have God-given talents as a girl."

As brash and confident as she is talking about fashion and her future — she wants to be a sideline reporter on television, if not market her own fashion creations —

Clement is equally so on the court. She sets wicked screens, makes flashy no-look passes, is demonic on defense, and is in perpetual motion.

But for her boundless energy, she had struggled mightily in 2000. With a two-year starter, Kellie Jolly, gone to the WNBA, Clement was the heir apparent at point guard. She stayed in Knoxville over the summer, dropped some weight, and improved her speed and quickness.

During a trek through Europe, she played beautifully, but her effectiveness waned once the real season started. By January, her shooting touch was gone, as was her confidence. In a four-game stretch, she committed a horrendous total of 19 turnovers and scored just nine points. Pat Summitt decided to make a change, moving Clement to shooting guard in lieu of Kara Lawson, a more controlled, tempo-conscious freshman.

"Ace was a trouper," Summitt said. "She handled it very, very well. ... I told her, 'How you handle this is very important. How do you feel?' She said, 'Fine.' It was not a lengthy discussion."

But Clement's numbers didn't improve. Against Kentucky in her first game at shooting guard, she missed all three of her shots and had three turnovers. In the next game, against North Carolina State, she had five turnovers. In a nationally televised game with Connecticut, she went 2 for 8 from the floor.

By the Southeastern Conference tournament, she was reeling. Her line over three games: 1 for 7 from the field, 10 rebounds, nine fouls, seven assists, six turnovers, one steal — and the kicker — two points.

"During the SEC, I really, really struggled," Clement said. "I tried to force too much. I just talked to myself and told myself, 'You have to relax.' Since then, it's worked."

In four NCAA tournament wins, she was a defensive catalyst, waving her arms and sliding from side to side as she mercilessly defended opposing guards. In the Mideast semifinal, she picked the pocket of Virginia's Renee Robinson, then collided with Robinson and was rewarded with two foul shots and a shiner under each eye.

In the regional title game, against Texas Tech, she took the court after carefully printing the words TAKE ME HOME on the white tape protecting her left ankle. On her right ankle she wrote, "THE NEW ME."

"It's just because I've been struggling as far as my offensive game goes," Clement said. "It's more mental. I just told my teammates that this is my dream season, to win a national championship in my hometown. To do that I've got to get back to my own me, to be myself and let the game come to me."

Final Four weekend marked Clement's second trip to Philadelphia of the season. In December, the Vols played at St. Joseph's in a game highlighted by nearly 150 screeching fans of Clement's, including her mother and father. Summitt scheduled the game with Clement, who scored 10 points and made five assists, in mind.

"I think being in Philadelphia and certainly having a chance to go back home and play, it was good for Ace to do that," Summitt said. "It reminded her how much she wanted to get back to Philly, and hopefully helped her understand that when you are in a competitive situation, you have to keep focused at the task at hand and not get distracted. She handled it well prior to that game. Certainly, we need her to this time."

"I told my mom, 'I'm not dealing with friends. I'm just taking care of my family,' " Clement said. "My friends can take care of themselves. I'm here to take care of business.

... They'll understand."

After strutting in celebration following the win over Texas Tech, Clement sprinted into the locker room and grabbed a pen. On the white board, she scribbled: "80 more minutes + 4 halves = a national championship."

"If you break it down, that's what it takes," the glamour girl said. "We have to stay focused."

— *Ashley McGeachy*

Vivian Stringer was happy to be home in Philadelphia. Her path home was long and often painful.

For Vivian Stringer, Little to Prove

For more than 25 years, Vivian Stringer's career as a basketball coach has intertwined with her personal life in a most public and often painful way.

Sketches of the venerated coach of Rutgers' Final Four team are often imprinted with the personal trials as well as professional triumphs: the sudden loss of a husband, a child left severely handicapped by spinal meningitis.

Stringer has long been lauded for being a portrait of courage. She will always inspire all parents, but especially single mothers, because of her relentless pursuit of what is best for her children.

Stringer has also gone where few women of color have, a path long recognized in black America. And her loyalty to Temple coach John Chaney, the friend and confidant who greeted Stringer with a bouquet of roses upon Rutgers' triumphant arrival in Philadelphia, is legend.

But lest we forget, Stringer's presence in the Final Four reconfirmed one indisputable fact: She is as accomplished a coach as there is in basketball, period.

ERIC MENCHER / Inquirer Staff Photographer

Vivian Stringer directed her Rutgers Scarlet Knights in their first practice at the First Union Center. Stringer became the first coach – men's or women's – to lead three different teams to the Final Four.

Summitt and Auriemma may have the championship trophies. Texas' Jody Conradt may have more victories. But no one has done what Stringer did — move into the Final Four with her third different program.

"We were just talking about this today. Vivian's taken three different teams to the Final Four, something no one else has done," Villanova coach Harry Perretta said. "That has to be recognized. That is an extraordinary feat."

Stringer built those Final Four programs — at tiny Cheyney State, expansive Iowa and cosmopolitan Rutgers — in three distinct locales and schools. The one constant was the Stringer game: a conservative, disciplined approach anchored in the belief that the defense always comes first.

"They rebound extremely well, and they play hard," said Muffet McGraw, the coach of Notre Dame. "But defense, that's their thing. They're tough to prepare for because they play a lot of different defenses, too. If you score, you're really going to earn it."

Never before had the Stringer defense received this amount of attention, likely because never before had it appeared to be this utterly impenetrable.

Rutgers didn't just defeat teams on the long road to Philadelphia. It took most to new depths offensively. The Knights started their postseason by holding Perretta's Villanova team to 32 points, a record low for the Big East tournament. They ended their quest for the Final Four by limiting a Georgia team used to scoring 80 points a game to 20 first-half points and a season low of 51 overall.

"They make other teams play ugly," Penn coach Kelly Greenberg said. "It's so similar to Chaney's team in that they don't do anything that really stands out, but you're under their handle the whole time."

McGraw agreed. "People said to me, 'Oh, what happened to Georgia, they played a bad game,' " the Irish coach said. "They didn't play a bad game. Rutgers' defense won that game."

Stringer's zone defense — known as the Venus Flytrap at Cheyney — long ago stopped being a surprise. The mystery is in the number of aliases it assumes. Is it man or matchup, trapping or pressing?

"What impresses me is the way that Vivian and her staff made adjustments," Greenberg said, recalling how easily Rutgers dismantled her alma mater, Holy Cross, in the early rounds. "As a young coach, I'm always told that's the key, and that's what Vivian's team does very well."

Stringer's game not only moves. It evolves. So says Yolanda Laney, an all-American on Stringer's Cheyney team that went to the first NCAA Final Four, in 1982.

"There's a big difference between then and now," Laney said. "Our offenses only had one out-of-bounds play, one simple stack. Now there are a bunch of new offenses."

And the defenses? "We never played matchup or man-to-man, but ran trapping and presses," Laney said. "At Cheyney, it was the basics. Now everything she runs is more complex. I understand it's because I'm used to Ms. Stringer's teams. But if you're not, it's like a foreign language. And if you don't figure it out early in the game, you're in trouble."

— *Claire Smith*

Penn State's Final Four appearance meant a homecoming for Portland and her mother, Margaret Muth, a longtime Broomall resident who, three years earlier, had moved to State College with her daughter.

Lions Coach Gives
Care to Her No. 1 Fan

She held court, high above the court. Before Penn State's first-round NCAA tournament game against Youngstown State at the Bryce Jordan Center, the woman everyone calls "Granny" entertained visitor after visitor in her skybox.

First-year assistant Michael Peck's mother, in town from Florida, stopped by to say hello. Then a former Nittany Lion, recently married. Then another woman, who commented on how pretty she looked in her blue-and-black sweater vest, black turtleneck, black pants and gold necklace with a #1 GRANDMA charm.

Granny, 78, took it all in, then waved like the queen of England when her daughter, Penn State coach Rene Portland, took the court less than four minutes before tip-off.

"Yes, I am the queen," she quipped unapologetically.

During player introductions, she clapped politely, a noiseless clap befitting her highness.

"I'm more nervous than she is," Granny said of her daughter. "I don't like these elimination games."

But she liked being there. The queen didn't always reign in State College. Three years ago, the queen was almost dead.

Margaret Muth lay on the floor of her Broomall home, five hours after her knees gave way beneath her. Sixty extra pounds hung on her tiny frame. Her knees were raw. She couldn't get up.

———

No one calls Muth by her given name. She's "Mother"

to her seven children, four girls and three boys ranging from 37 to 55 years old, all born and raised in that house in Broomall. She's "Granny" to her 17 grandchildren and three great-grandchildren, and to whomever else she meets, regardless of their age.

But on that winter day, in solitude, she was stripped bare. That day, she was Margaret Muth.

Some days later, with Muth resting in the hospital, her children discussed how best to care for their ailing mother. Not only was she a diabetic who was not taking her medicine or eating well, but she had Parkinson's disease and was living alone. She rebuffed visitors and asked her children to call her, but not stop by the house. Instead of fixing dinner for herself, she'd grab the nearest bag of candy, sit in her favorite chair, and watch television.

"Her whole life has been about taking care of everyone but herself," Portland said.

Portland's siblings unanimously voted to put their mother in a retirement home, but Portland would have none of it. When she was a child, one of her great-aunts lost both her legs, and lived with the Muths before moving to a nursing home. Portland visited occasionally, and the antiseptic odor of that home was imprinted in her memory.

"It would smell, and it was sad," Portland said. "That's my memory of those kind of places."

Portland learned that there are three phases of retirement homes: first a small apartment, then a semi-care facility, and finally a nursing home. Her siblings said a retirement community would be perfect for their mother because she could take the bus to nearby outlet malls and play bingo, and they could visit frequently.

"I don't think anybody really understood that my mother was past phase one, was somewhat in phase two, and if we didn't do something, she'd be real close to phase three," Portland said. "When my brothers and sisters called me and told me they had found the perfect place, from Day 1, I said, 'It's not going to happen. She's going to come live with me.' "

At halftime, the Lions led Youngstown State, 36-21, but the Penguins scored 10 of the last 11 points of the half to make it more of a game than Granny would have liked. It wasn't enough to send her scurrying beneath the bleachers to say a rosary, the way she did when Portland was a player at Immaculata, but still, she was nervous and fidgety.

"I've got my hands together," Granny said, still planted in her throne. "I didn't like those points at the end. I didn't like that at all, especially in these elimination games."

Granny has seen her share of basketball games. Portland played for Cathy Rush at Immaculata from 1972 to '75, and won three national titles and 85 of 90 games.

One of the early losses came in a nearly empty gym in Philadelphia. It was disturbingly quiet, and afterward Portland's parents blamed the atmosphere for the loss. Her father, who owned a hardware store in Upper Darby, went to the shop and got five dozen metal buckets. He and Granny lugged them to every game thereafter, and if the Mighty Macs trailed at halftime, out came the buckets. The noise was deafening.

Once, the Muths got in a car accident en route to a game and foisted the buckets on a passerby who was also headed to the game. Another time, they schemed with the Immaculata cheerleaders to smuggle the buckets into Madison Square Garden. The 1975 national title game between the Macs and Delta State was delayed because

Delta State obtained a court order barring the buckets from the game. Immaculata lost.

"When we got there, it was a nothing school," Granny said of Immaculata. "The players were nothing. Their coach was nothing. We didn't know what a regional was. We didn't know anything. We had to wash the uniforms, travel ourselves. We had to do everything. They called us the Cinderella school. But we had the buckets."

Granny watches Nittany Lions football games from the press box at Beaver Stadium. Before games, she goes with Rene and her husband, John, to a tailgate party, where her favorite Lions player, Helen Darling, always stops by. Darling scouts the table of food for Granny, takes her order — usually something sweet — then sneaks her a piece of cake.

"We just respect Granny," Darling said. "Everyone has a hug or kiss for her. ... That's Rene's mother. She took Granny in and is working" 24 hours a day, seven days a week. "She comes to practice, then goes home and takes care of her. We respect that."

Said Ellen Perry, Penn State associate athletic director: "Penn State has a family orientation, and Granny is as much a part of what happens here as anyone else. She's a critical part of the basketball operation, just because she's Granny."

And she's an integral part of the Portland household. Portland wakes up every day at 5 a.m., goes to Mass, then returns home to care for Granny. She bathes and feeds her. Some mornings are better than others, but these days there are more good than bad.

Granny has lost 60 pounds. Her medicine has been consolidated, and she no longer takes the insulin she needed three years ago. She had one knee replaced two years ago, will have the other replaced this summer, and has traded in her wheelchair for a cane.

"It's been hectic, and it's a challenge," John Portland said. "But she's a lot of fun, and the kids are real good with her, too. That's a plus. ... Before, she was in that big house, and we felt sorry being this far away."

Granny's humor sneaks up on you; you don't think that someone so seemingly frail could be so funny. Her wit is quick, even if her delivery isn't.

A day after joining John at the Nittany Lions men's basketball team's first-round NIT game at the Bryce Jordan Center, she was asked which team was better, the men's or women's. She declined to answer. "I'll have the Crispin brothers all over me if I say," she said.

Granny's throne in the Portland house is a chair in the living room. She has a toll-free telephone line that her grandchildren use liberally. And she's constantly entertained by Portland's three children. Christine, a Penn State graduate who played for her mother, often calls from Philadelphia; John, a Penn State junior, stops by. Stephen, a junior in high school, dressed Granny in Mexican garb for Halloween. "She got a load of candy," he said.

"People say, 'I'll never do that to my children,' " Portland said of caring for her mother. "Well, you know what? I'm glad my mother did this to me. ... To me, this is 'death do us part.' My mother and I, she will live in my home until she goes to sleep. I know it's hard on my brothers and sisters, but we're going to deal with it."

With 2 minutes, 8 seconds left in the game, Granny conceded victory. The Lions led Youngstown State, 79-56, so there was no need for a novena.

"They're going to win," she said. "That means we play Sunday."

When Penn State advanced to the Final Four in Philadelphia, Granny had a front-row seat at the First Union Center. "She gets my first ticket," Portland said.

When asked how special it would be for Portland and Penn State to play in Philadelphia, Granny paused. "I don't know if they'd recognize her," she said.

Everyone would recognize Granny, perched on her throne, wearing Penn State's colors and waving to her daughter. It's hard to miss the queen.

— *Ashley McGeachy*

On the court, it was hard to miss Connecticut junior Shea Ralph. Her path to the Final Four began in Fayetteville, N.C., and included dual knee surgeries and a rough freshman year.

Ralph's Passion Is Not Concealed

Shea Ralph's game face burns with a look that is equal parts desperation and fury. The Connecticut all-American's eyes narrow until they fix an opponent with frightening intensity. Her lips curl into a snarl. The nostrils flare and her blond ponytail flails menacingly from side to side like a whip.

It is no mask. Ralph, the 6-foot swing player who is the spiritual leader of this team, is a relentless competitor, bursting into passing lanes, finishing on the break, taking the charge. Her style suggests not only a desire to win, but a need.

"What drives her comes from inside," said LSU coach Sue Gunter, after Connecticut defeated the Tigers in the

first all-American basketball player. She lives in Florida now, still working hard, saving her money to take several trips a year to watch her daughter play.

"She let me play all the sports I wanted to play, but she steered me toward basketball," Ralph said. "And once I picked up on that and wanted to do that more than anything, she just took my hand and guided me."

And that road eventually led to Connecticut.

"I'm going to miss a lot when I'm done here," Ralph said. "I'm going to miss this place like I don't think I've ever missed anything. But I'm going to be very happy to have had this experience. I think it made me a much better person."

And Connecticut a much better team.

— *Frank Fitzpatrick*

Certainly not every player or every coach was from Philadelphia. But Summitt, born and bred in Tennessee, was truly an outsider.

Vols Almost Intruders in Philadelphia Final Four

Just as Tony Curtis never presumed to upstage Cary Grant, just as Dean and Sammy always dutifully bowed to the Chairman of the Board, most everyone involved with women's basketball has long understood that Tennessee and star billing are usually as synonymous as, well, the University of Tennessee and national championships.

Usually.

A phenomenon stranger than a two-year stretch without a Tennessee title unfolded in the days leading up to the women's Final Four's first round. Because there was such a

strong Philadelphia presence in the other teams, it was as if Tennessee had gone from scene-stealer to scenic background.

Tennessee's celebrated coach, Pat Summitt, may be the owner of six NCAA championships, including three of the last four, but she understood that for all her successes, this weekend wasn't about a coach who is as Southern as a Tennessee waltz or as consistently brilliant as her current dynasty. Being as Philadelphian as cream cheese was the big theme of the Philly-style Final Four.

So Summitt accepted with grace and humor these Philly Games. She watched as her counterparts commanded star turns, beginning with Vivian Stringer, the former Cheyney State coach who led Rutgers against Summitt's

ERIC MENCHER / Inquirer Staff Photographer

Tuning up for their Final Four showdown with Rutgers, Tennessee's players focused on dribbling drills at the First Union Center. From left: Tamika Catchings, Kristen Clement, Kyra Elzy and Amanda Canon.

Vols in the first national semifinal. Then there was Geno Auriemma, the Connecticut coach who is from Norristown, and Penn State's Rene Portland of Broomall.

Those coaches not named Summitt were having their moment not just because they are talented, as shown by Auriemma's being named Associated Press coach of the year or Stringer's record third big show with three different programs. They also possessed impeccable timing, not to mention the good sense to put their signature on a tournament that just happened to unfold in their hometown.

If that were not enough, one, and possibly two, women who surpassed Wilt Chamberlain's Philadelphia Public League scoring record were waiting to break Summitt's heart, or at least steal the spotlight.

"They've had it in the past; they can share it, now," said Shawnetta Stewart, the University City graduate and Rutgers' leading scorer who, along with Penn State's Andrea Garner, passed The Stilt in the record book.

Talk about a closed club.

"I'm just glad we have Ace Clement, because now all four teams have Philadelphia ties," Summitt said, smiling.

Now, understand that media outlets were dutifully lining up when the only thing that was clear was that Connecticut and Tennessee were about the only locks to make it to Philadelphia.

Still, when Penn State and Rutgers grabbed the last two slots with regional championships, well, let's just say local as well as national interest jumped to a whole new level.

According to tournament organizers, the phones at NCAA central began jangling the moment Portland's Nittany Lions crashed a party once seemingly reserved for top seeds. The calls picked up momentum when Rutgers did the same, causing a bump in requests for credentials, interviews, even tickets that were no longer available.

"That's what the Northeast does to you," said Cathy Andruzzi, executive director of Philadelphia Women's Basketball 2000. "We always said that if there were times when women's basketball jumped to the next level, it was 1995, when Connecticut won the national championship. The game took a big shot in the arm. Now we've reached that next level with a Northeast school and the Northeast media in the fourth-largest media market in the country."

Again, Tennessee — the team that consistently plays to

packed houses and travels the land treated like rock-star royalty — initially had something to do with all this. But the Vols didn't have everything to do with it. This time, it was Rocky Top that was caught in a shadow, the one being cast by the Delaware Valley.

To its credit, the Tennessee contingent not only recognized the phenomenon, but fully understood, because Pat Summitt fully understood.

"I've told our team that it's a local flavor; all three coaches have Philadelphia ties," said Summitt. "We've been to four Final Fours and we've been the top dog. We've been the underdog, too. So we're just proud to be here.

"We can't concern ourselves with what everyone else is thinking or who the favorite team might be. I don't think this team feels the pressures that a lot of other teams that have been in the Final Four have felt. Now, will that influence our play in a positive? You hope it will, but you don't know until they throw the basketball up."

History shows that when they throw the basketball up in an NCAA tournament game featuring Tennessee, it is the Vols who feel at home, no matter what the locale. "I told [the team] let's go out, have fun, play Tennessee basketball — and that's what I expect them to do," Summitt said.

— *Claire Smith*

That's what Auriemma wanted, too. Don't worry about Penn State's Helen Darling or Andrea Garner, he told his players. Focus on Huskies basketball.

UConn Just Worries About Its Own Game

With all the success that his Connecticut teams have enjoyed over the last 12 years, Geno Auriemma knows what it takes to prepare his team for the next game, especially in the pressurized atmosphere of the women's Final Four. Sometimes, though, details about the opponent's roster seem to be a bit fuzzy.

Penn State was the Huskies' foe in the second game of the NCAA semifinal doubleheader at the First Union Center. The day before the game, Auriemma talked about how well the Lions played as a team, saying that they had seven seniors on their roster.

Uh, Penn State had just three seniors on its roster, and one, Marissa Graby, had played only 194 minutes in 27 games.

That was a small mistake, though, considering how Auriemma got his team ready for a critical game. Shea Ralph tried to shed some light on the way the Huskies prepared.

"I think you'll find that, with our team, we do look at the things [opponents] do on offense and defense," Ralph said, "but we don't really concentrate on that. We are more focused on what we're doing as opposed to how we are going to beat what they are doing.

"I think, if we just stick with our game and be confident and play hard, then things will work out for us."

The Huskies, the 1995 NCAA champions, were playing in their fourth Final Four but their first since 1996. They breezed through the East Regional, winning four games by an average of 36.5 points.

The Lions, meanwhile, were in a Final Four for the first time in their history, but they were pushed hard during their run. They made 11 of 13 free throws down the stretch to beat Auburn in the second round, and they grabbed a one-point semifinal win over Iowa State, thanks to Helen Darling's steal and basket with 12 seconds to play.

In the regional final, however, they posted a remarkably easy 86-65 victory over Louisiana Tech. And although they entered the UConn game as the underdogs, they didn't feel like underdogs, even though many anticipated a renewal of the sport's hottest rivalry — the one between Connecticut and Tennessee — in the national championship.

"I haven't heard too much about it," Penn State's Andrea Garner said. "I know we're not going to let them get there easily. We have a game plan, and we're going to execute it and hope to use it to our advantage."

The Huskies had been a dominant team all season, and in this, their 12th consecutive NCAA tournament, they were averaging 96.8 points. They had a different high scorer in each of their four tournament games. Their bench had outscored the opposing bench to the tune of 151-48.

For the season, UConn was 14-1 against ranked opponents, including an 87-74 victory over Penn State on Dec. 5 in the Honda Elite 4 tournament in Orlando, Fla.

"This is March, and it's different," Ralph said. "Everybody has gotten better."

Lions coach Rene Portland was encouraged by the play of Garner, her 6-foot-3 center, and Maren Walseth, a 6-3 forward, in the UConn game in December. The two combined for 42 points while shooting 17 for 35 from the field.

Portland was quoted afterward that the Lions' inside game had "killed" that of the Huskies. Before the national semifinal, she contended that she had been misquoted, and she noted that Tamika Williams, a 6-2 UConn sophomore, had missed the game with a stress fracture in her left foot.

"I think we did a very good job of attacking the post area," Portland said. "We had a lot of high-low combinations. They had an injury at that position, so we were able to take advantage of that."

A key matchup involved Darling, a senior, and UConn's Sue Bird, a sophomore. They were two of the four nominees for the Nancy Lieberman-Cline Award, which is given to the nation's outstanding point guard.

"They have two different functions, I think," Auriemma said. "Sue Bird is kind of like a classic player. You can't put a label on her. She's like the old-fashioned guard who does all the things she needs to do. Helen Darling is a senior, and Sue is really playing her first year in college. It will be interesting to see how they handle the pressure of being out there."

— Joe Juliano

Just as playing their own game would be a key for the Huskies, Tennessee would need a big game from its star — Tamika Catchings. The daughter of a former 76er, she had been waiting her entire career to star in the big game.

For Catchings, Goal Is in Sight

Writhing on the floor, Tamika Catchings shrieked in agony, but her father, his long legs crossed in front of him as he sat in the stands, did not move. He didn't wince as his daughter lay on her back, her stellar season in jeopardy, although everyone else in the Memphis Pyramid was breathless, fearing that Tennessee's star forward had suffered a serious ankle injury.

Harvey Catchings knew better. His daughter wanted to go to Philadelphia for the Final Four almost as badly as he did, and nothing, certainly not a sprained ankle, would keep her from leading the Volunteers past Texas Tech to get there.

"She wants to win this thing," he said as Tennessee prepared to face Rutgers in the first game of the national semifinals. "Do you understand? She wants to win."

Of course she did. After all, she is his daughter: the little girl who roller-bladed on the streets of Italy while he played professional basketball; the girl who grew up to be tough, talented, driven and, as a junior at Tennessee, hellbent on getting back to the national championship game.

For Harvey Catchings, 49 years old and a mortgage banker at Chase Manhattan in Chicago, coming back to Philadelphia meant a trip to Bookbinder's for seafood, frivolity, and reminiscing about his days as a 76er. A third-round draft pick by the team out of Hardin-Simmons University in Abilene, Texas, the 6-foot-10 Catchings played in Philadelphia from 1974 to '79, averaging 5.0 rebounds, 3.0 points and 1.6 blocks per game.

He was part of the storied 1976-77 team that, with Julius Erving, Doug Collins and Mike Dunleavy, went to the NBA Finals before losing the series to Portland, four games to two. That team spawned some terrifically talented progeny: tennis phenom Alexandra Stevenson, former Duke guard Chris Collins, current Blue Devil Mike Dunleavy Jr., and Tamika Catchings, this season's women's Naismith player of the year, and her sister, Tauja, who had just completed a four-year career at Illinois.

All Tamika remembers about her father's 11-year professional career, which included stints in Milwaukee, New Jersey, Los Angeles and Italy, is what she's seen on tapes — blooper tapes. "Poor daddy," she said. "He once scored a basket for the other team."

With her father, mother Wanda and sister among the

many family members scheduled to attend, Tamika was back in the Final Four with a shot at her second national title since arriving at Tennessee. Unlike in 1998, when the Vols beat Louisiana Tech to win Pat Summitt's sixth NCAA championship, this team belonged to Tamika. She, not the famed Chamique Holdsclaw, was the go-to player, the one who dazzled spectators with her ability to seemingly be everywhere at once, blocking shots on the perimeter, gliding through the lane for finger-roll layups, snagging rebounds along the baseline.

Despite facing physical defenses all season, she had averaged a team-high 15.7 points and 7.9 rebounds. She had raised her game in the NCAA tournament, leading all participants in rebounding (10.8), and ranking fourth in scoring (17.5) and sixth in blocks (2.3).

"Tamika Catchings is exactly what you'd think. She's a warrior," Summitt said. "It's interesting how people have matched up on her this year. ... She's had people shove her in the back, forearm her, and really come out physical. She's handled it well. At times I think I'm more upset about it than she is."

Added Harvey Catchings: "Her best attribute is her heart. She goes out to win at all costs, whatever it takes. It's always giving 110 percent, if that's possible. Whatever the team needs at that point in the game, she sacrifices and gives it."

But the soft-spoken, easy-going Tamika is low-key about her skills. Her passion is unmistakable, but she sounds almost apologetic when she talks about her accomplishments, and she refuses to compare her game to that of Holdsclaw, widely considered one of the greatest women's basketball players ever. Holdsclaw, last season's WNBA rookie of the year with the Washington Mystics, led

Tennessee to three consecutive national championships, from 1996 to '98, and was the program's all-time career leader in scoring, field goals, free throws and rebounds.

Tamika scored the most points in a season by a Tennessee freshman (averaging 18.2) and the second most, behind Holdsclaw, as a sophomore (16.6).

"A lot of people will say what they want to, but I'm not trying to be the next Chamique Holdsclaw," she said. "That was never my goal."

— *Ashley McGeachy*

With so much hype, tickets to the sold-out event were scarce, and expensive.

The Hottest Ticket in Town

Think of something that's hard to find: World peace. Free cable TV. A low-calorie cheesesteak.

Now consider this: It would have been easier to get any of those things than it would be to scrounge up a ticket for the NCAA women's basketball Final Four tournament for less than $350 or so.

"It's as hot a ticket as I've seen in a while," said John Page, senior vice president and general manager of the First Union Center. "This is like an NBA or NHL playoff game in terms of demand, or an 'N Sync concert."

Such was the sizzle generated by the four teams with ties to Philadelphia — Penn State, Rutgers, Connecticut and Tennessee — in a sport that had been gaining fans and popularity year after year.

Beyond the hometown ties of coaches and players, the tournament had inspired higher-than-normal demand from the NCAA's corporate partners, because many of the companies are located in the Northeast, said Donna Noonan, vice president of NCAA Division I Women's Basketball.

"Oh, a ticket to this thing is beyond hot, beyond hot," said Cathy Andruzzi, executive director of Philadelphia Women's Basketball 2000. "I have a lot more friends today than I did yesterday, all asking for tickets."

Officially, the tournament was sold out in July, when the NCAA held a lottery to sell about 6,000 tickets to the general public at a cost of $90 each, according to Sue Donohoe, director of Division I women's basketball. Total capacity for the tournament was roughly 16,770. Each ticket was for a seat at the two semifinal games and the championship game.

Each team received 700 tickets each, going mostly to the teams themselves, school administrators, season-ticket holders, big-time donors, and students, officials said. The association of basketball coaches got 3,000 tickets, and the remaining 5,000 or so were divided among members of the NCAA and the local organizing committee, Donohoe said.

So, if all of the general tickets were sold two to a customer by lottery, and all of the remaining tickets were divvied up, how come brokers in New Jersey and on the Internet had tickets for which they were demanding $350 a pop?

In a word, capitalism.

"Keep in mind, when the whole tournament started, there were people who bought tickets for the Final Four with the hope that their team would be in it," explained Barry Lefkowitz, executive director of the East Coast Ticket Brokers Association in Burlington. "As their teams became eliminated, they had no reason to go. So they turned around and sold to a broker. And believe me, they turned a profit."

— *Alfred Lubrano*

Four of the most talented teams in the country made it to Philadelphia. And they were ready to prove who was best.

CHARLES FOX / Inquirer Staff Photographer

Rutgers fans Kasheef (left) and Linda McCalla made sure they came early to cheer for the Scarlet Knights at the First Union Center. Rutgers took on Tennessee in the first game of the national semifinals.

Chapter 6

The Final Four

With the First Union Center packed with the largest crowd to ever witness a college basketball game in Pennsylvania, it was time to play ball. The scene was festive, inside and outside the building.

Final Four Scene Really Is Madness

Penn State assistant coach Michael Peck was seated on press row at the First Union Center to scout the opening game between Tennessee and Rutgers before his team played Connecticut.

The building was packed. The sellout crowd of 20,060 was the largest ever to watch a college basketball game — men's or women's — in the state. The previous record was 19,372 at the First Union Center for a men's game on Feb. 16, 1997, between Villanova and Notre Dame.

Peck looked around at the crowd as pep bands blared before the tip-off.

"It's just madness," he said, smiling.

Well before the game began, activities both inside and

outside the building had a feeling of frenzy.

Hundreds of fans outside the building — many dressed in Tennessee orange or blue-and-white Connecticut shirts, hats and face paint, walked along holding their hands up, with their fingers in the shape of the letter V.

RON CORTES / Inquirer Staff Photographer

Charles Cassidy, 81, of New Brunswick, N.J., came to the First Union Center to make some noise for his favorite team: Rutgers.

No, they weren't predicting victory for their teams.

Instead, they were indicating the number two, as in "Need two tickets."

Reselling tickets is illegal, however, and representatives of the city department of licensing and inspection, as well as Philadelphia police, were close by, monitoring the scene.

New Jersey Gov. Christie Whitman was in the house to cheer for Rutgers, while Pennsylvania Gov. Tom Ridge was present to give his support to Penn State.

Former tennis stars Billie Jean King and Martina Navratilova were among the celebrity guests from the sports and entertainment world.

Former Mayor Edward G. Rendell was in the crowd, as was local legend Dawn Staley of the U.S. national team, and her teammate Lisa Leslie of the WNBA's Los Angeles

Sparks. Cynthia Cooper of the three-time WNBA champion Houston Comets was also among the stars from the women's pro league.

Most of the corporate suites, however, had a family-style flavor as fans munched on pizza, popcorn, and liquid refreshments prior to the start of play.

Immaculata, the alma mater of Penn State coach Rene Portland, was represented by 12 nuns, including the past and current presidents of the school.

Unseen by most of the spectators in a room behind the stands, a huge contingent of news media members jockeyed for position to file their stories later in the night.

According to Comcast-Spectacor spokesman Ike Richman, 669 press credentials had been issued.

"It's more than when we had the Stanley Cup finals in 1997 or the United States figure skating championships in 1998," Richman said.

"There's a lot of magic here in this Final Four I have not seen in any others," said Hall of Famer Ann Meyers. "Philadelphia has done an unbelievable job getting ready for this. The media has been so supportive. I just got off a local TV broadcast. Where else do they have a roundtable breaking down the women's game?

"Someone said they're really overdoing this women's game.

"Overdoing it? It's about time. What are they doing with the men's game?"

Peter Luukko, president of the First Union Center, said, "When we bid for this event, the Center wasn't even built. We had to bid on it based on the Spectrum, but we would have had to add seats. It would have cost $1 million, so I'm glad they got this up and running.

"The magnitude of this event has just become grand.

We're on national TV, so that makes it great for the city as well. It's become better than we could even have imagined."

One fan, Patty Marshall, came from Anchorage, Alaska.

"I came from a long way, but I'm happy to be here," she said. "I've never even been to the East Coast before. I'm a big basketball fan and I ordered tickets when I saw they would be available."

Bill Miller, a Rutgers fan from Buffalo, said, "I'm breaking my string of six consecutive men's Final Fours to come here. I went to Rutgers, so that's why I'm here. I hope my young daughters — 9 and 4 years old — will eventually play ball there."

— *Mel Greenberg*

After months of planning and raising money and hours of practice and games, the ball was finally tossed up at center court. The games had begun.

Volunteers Shake Off Rutgers in Second Half

As the first fans trickled into the First Union Center for the NCAA women's semifinals, Kristen Clement sat on the bench with Tennessee assistant Al Brown, the man she considers a father. Her hand wrapped in his, she listened as Brown reviewed the game plan.

"Play with an attitude," Brown told her.

Play like Ace.

The Volunteers exuded an attitude of defiance against Rutgers. They were composed during a first half in which they struggled against Rutgers' unconventional matchup

RON CORTES / Inquirer Staff Photographer

Kristen Clement showed her emotions in Tennessee's tussle with Rutgers in the national semifinals. The Volunteers guard helped her team to a 64-54 victory. It would be her final game of the season.

JERRY LODRIGUSS / Inquirer Staff Photographer

Tennessee's Semeka Randall hit the deck at the foul line as Rutgers' Davalyn Cunningham tried for a steal. The Vols put the game away with clutch free-throw shooting down the stretch.

zone and, after finally forcing the tempo to their liking, they beat the Knights, 64-54, to advance to the NCAA title game.

"Clearly, I felt as the game wore on, we became a more determined basketball team," Pat Summitt said afterward. "We focused less on what we didn't do and more on what we needed to do."

A mere 28-26 halftime lead? No problem. The Vols' star player scoreless through the opening 19 minutes? Big deal. A determined Rutgers team that outrebounded them by 7-0 to start the second half? No problem.

Many of the players on Tennessee's team already had won one NCAA title. They had an attitude, and they were poised.

Behind savvy play from freshman point guard Kara Lawson, the Vols dissected Rutgers' defense. The 5-foot-9 Lawson did in the second half what was unthinkable in the first — she scored inside. At will.

And by being a perimeter threat, too, she freed the fantastic Tamika Catchings to work her wonders. When Catchings scored on a driving layup to give Tennessee a 47-39 lead with 8 minutes, 28 seconds remaining in the game, she and Lawson had 17 of the Vols' 19 second-half points.

After Rutgers reserve Linda Miles scored to pull the Knights to within 49-45 with 6:40 left, Tennessee calmly made 13 of 16 free throws in the final 6:25 to seal its 33d victory of the season.

The unflappable Lawson finished with 19 points, three assists, one block, one steal and no turnovers in 35 minutes. She changed the tempo of the game, and validated Summitt's midseason decision to move her from shooting guard to point guard, the position formerly held by

Clement. And she did it playing with a chronically sore back.

"Kara Lawson deserves an awful lot of credit for the position that we put people in," Summitt said. "... I thought she just did an excellent job of breaking down the defense and running our offense."

Said Lawson: "I like playing in the Final Four, and I like playing on this stage, and I like playing in a tournament where you know if you lose, you go home. And so I think our team likes this type of atmosphere. I think our team thrives in this type of situation."

Catchings added 13 points — 11 in the second half — and 12 rebounds for her sixth career double-double in NCAA tournament action.

She credited Lawson with the win. "She did it all for us," Catchings said. "She stepped up her game definitely, just driving and penetrating in, penetrating the gaps. That's what we really needed."

Rutgers, which finished the season 26-8, scored its fewest points in the last 14 games. Shawnetta Stewart, Tasha Pointer and Linda Miles each scored 11 points and were the only Knights in double figures.

After upsetting Georgia to reach coach Vivian Stringer's third Final Four and the school's first, the Knights traveled from Portland, Ore., back to New Jersey. After arriving in Philadelphia, the pace was frenetic, and it took its toll, Stringer said.

"We got in at the last second and have been hopping ever since," she said. Against Tennessee, "We were a little tight."

One player in particular wasn't: Clement, who had struggled throughout the postseason.

In a psychological ploy, she had been writing "THE

JERRY LODRIGUSS / Inquirer Staff Photographer
Tennessee's Michelle Snow wrested a rebound away from
Rutgers' Shawnetta Stewart, who scored 11 points in her finale.

NEW ME" on the tape encasing her right ankle. Until this game, it had failed.

But in her homecoming, with her team struggling early against Rutgers' discombobulating zone, Clement buried three quick jumpers, including two three-pointers, to give the Vols an early 10-5 lead. She was relegated to the bench after picking up her second foul with 13:22 remaining, but her impact was felt.

"She was awesome," Brown said. "She'd been in such a slump."

"He's like a father to me," Clement said of Brown. "He calms me down."

And, for a night, he inspired her to exude an attitude.

— *Ashley McGeachy*

Tamika Catchings had a troubling night, thanks to a constant swarm of Scarlet Knights defenders. Yet in the end, she broke free.

Catchings Comes Through in the Clutch

"Take it out of her hand, Kourtney, that skinny thing!"

Not even Rutgers fans at the First Union Center had the proper respect for Tamika Catchings, the Tennessee forward who was merely the national player of the year.

The woman from the Scarlet Knights' cheering section yelled out as reserve Kourtney Walton was on the ground, scrambling for a ball with Catchings, just after a shot by Catchings had hit the front rim early in the semifinal.

One axiom of the matchup zone practiced by Vivian Stringer's team — Temple Owls fans know it well — is: Don't let the opponent's star beat you.

CHARLES FOX / Inquirer Staff Photographer

In a scramble for a loose ball, Michelle Snow of the
Volunteers fought to keep her balance as the Scarlet Knights'
Tasha Pointer fell.

For most of the evening, Catchings got caught-in-a-traffic-jam treatment from Rutgers. For all her fluid talents, she is the kind of player who lets the game come to her.

The game stayed at arm's length for a while. Catchings had just two points at halftime, and those two came in the final minute of the first half. The Vols held a tenuous 28-26 lead at the half.

"We played on our heels, and sometimes I can help and sometimes I can't," Catchings said.

At the break, Summitt said she looked at Catchings and Semeka Randall, who had three points, and said, "This is life for the all-Americans. People key on you. They double-team you. You have to learn to do other things, and you have to be more aggressive. You have to hit open teammates when that happens."

Walking onto the court after intermission, Clement said to Catchings, "Let's start over. We've got a new half."

Eventually, Catchings got her points, 12 in the second half, and Tennessee survived. But for the longest time, Rutgers wasn't giving her an inch. Sometimes the Scarlet Knights were taking an inch. One time, Rutgers forward Linda Miles wrapped her arms around Catchings before an inbounds pass: Don't even think about trying to make a highlight here.

This was a give-and-take relationship, though. Catchings had her elbows out and swinging when she grabbed rebounds. She drew two crucial Rutgers charges in the second half.

As Rutgers lost a little energy, Catchings started demanding the ball more. Not right away, however. In fact, early in the second half, she tried to force the issue a little too much. From about 18 feet away, she feinted toward the hoop and pulled back and shot a jumper over Rutgers star Shawnetta Stewart. Air ball. Then Stewart beat her downcourt by a couple of steps and got the ball for a fastbreak layup to give Rutgers a 32-30 lead three minutes into the second half. Catchings shook her head, taking responsibility for Stewart's play. Then she hit a turnaround 16-footer right away at the other end to tie the game.

And then she elevated her game. She was doing her part on the defensive end. One possession, Tennessee was in a 2-3 zone, the next a 1-3-1 zone. Then the Vols went to man-to-man. It wasn't like there was only one team playing defense out there. Catchings would run the back of a 1-3-1, stay back in Tennessee's full-court zone pressure, and be up trying to cause havoc in the press.

Her offensive contributions were huge. She caught a rebound in the air and put the ball back before she hit the ground to tie the game. When Rutgers drew within two with 12 minutes left, Catchings hit a three-pointer from up top. The Scarlet Knights never got that close again — to Tennessee or its star.

— *Mike Jensen*

Stringer's homecoming ended one game early. Her face told the story.

Stringer's Moment on Center Stage

Vivian Stringer had hoped to savor every aspect of her Rutgers team's visit to the women's Final Four.

The sights. The sounds. The city.

The competition. The crowds. The camaraderie of her players.

In the first game of the national semifinals at the First

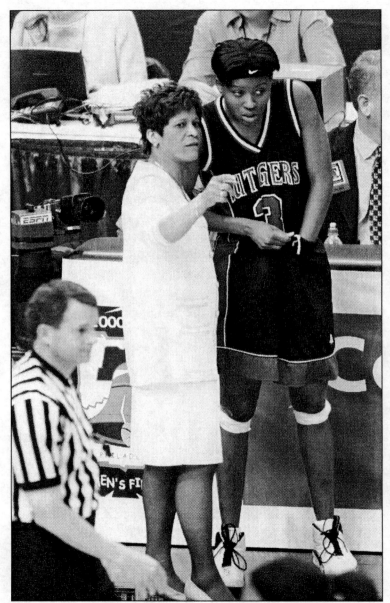

JERRY LODRIGUSS / Inquirer Staff Photographer

Rutgers coach Vivian Stringer gave direction to guard Usha Gilmore during the first half. "I'm proud of my team," Stringer said after the loss to the Vols.

Union Center, Stringer had some moments to remember, but also some she and the Scarlet Knights would sooner forget as they fell one game short of a berth in the title game.

These were the highlights of Stringer's evening as the coach, dressed smartly in white skirt and matching jacket, worked the sideline against another giant of the women's game, Tennessee's Pat Summitt:

7:09 p.m.: After player introductions, Stringer shares a warm embrace with Summitt; the midcourt meeting brings together more than 50 years of head coaching experience and 1,300 victories. It is hard to imagine two better ambassadors for the women's game anywhere.

7:14: "Push it. Push it. Push it," Stringer commands junior point guard Tasha Pointer after a rebound by center Tammy Sutton-Brown triggers a Scarlet Knights fastbreak opportunity. "Push it," she yells as Pointer weaves her way through traffic and past the hash mark in front of the Scarlet Knights' bench.

7:27: Once, twice, three times Stringer pumps her fist on the bench after a defensive stand by the Scarlet Knights forces the Volunteers into a shot-clock violation. Aggressive defense always has been a trademark of Stringer-coached teams, whether it was at her first coaching stop at Cheyney State, her second at Iowa, or this one with the Scarlet Knights. Two more first-half stops also produced similar reactions.

7:44: Head thrown back, hands to her face, it's agony for Stringer to watch Rutgers charged with a turnover as Pointer and junior center Linda Miles share possession of a defensive rebound.

7:47: "Hands. Hands. Hands," Stringer shouts, arms upraised above her head as Tennessee probes the Scarlet

Knights' defense.

7:53: "That's a foul," Stringer screeches to no one in particular after Volunteers center Michelle Snow bumps Sutton-Brown on a put-back attempt down low. With less than three minutes to play in the first half, it is the first time that Stringer, who leaves her seat on the bench only on occasion, appears to notice the officials on the floor — except for the few instances when she leans left or right to look past one positioned in her line of sight.

7:58: After Shawnetta Stewart is whistled for a reach-in foul with 0.6 seconds left in the first half, Stringer has her first words for an official. They are spirited, but brief. Tennessee takes a 28-26 halftime lead as Semeka Randall makes one of two free throws.

8:31: Calm and collected, Stringer signals for a time-out after a gorgeous pass by Kristen Clement finds Snow alone underneath. The cross-court look not only catches the Scarlet Knights napping, it also gives the Volunteers an easy basket and a 40-36 lead.

8:41: Stringer, trying to stem an 11-3 Tennessee run, claps encouragement after the fourth foul on Randall sends Stewart to the line for a one-and-one. The senior forward makes one of two, ending a scoreless stretch that spanned 4 minutes, 9 seconds.

8:45: "Come on," Stringer yells, reacting to an offensive foul called on Stewart in the low post.

8:49: With a single stomp of her foot, Stringer shows she can't believe Volunteers guard Kara Lawson found a way to escape a Scarlet Knights trap in the backcourt. "Hands," she says. "Hands."

8:56: Hand on chin, Stringer whispers to assistant coach Jolette Law, who is seated to her left. Law nods in agreement: Rutgers must find a way to climb out of a nine-point deficit, 54-45.

8:59: For only the second time all night, Stringer finds fault with an official's call. She is up off her seat after forward Kourtney Walton is bumped underneath with no whistle. "Come on," Stringer says before returning to her chair. "Come on."

9:05: Stringer joins in the applause as fan-favorite Stewart leaves the floor with her fifth foul.

9:07: Stringer is still coaching, still pushing, even with her team down by 62-52 with 45.1 seconds to play. A Rutgers time-out sets up a play for the Knights' next possession.

9:11: It's over. Stringer, frozen stoically and silently on the bench for seconds after the final buzzer, rises to shake hands with Summitt after the Volunteers clinch a berth in the final. Stringer walks quietly to the locker room, head bowed.

9:50: "Coach Stringer helped make me the player and the person I am today," Stewart says.

9:55: "I'm proud of my team because they do learn and they do remember," Stringer says. "Hopefully, next time, we will give a better accounting of ourselves."

— *Jay Nagle*

In the second game, Penn State hung with UConn into the second half before the Huskies pulled away.

Relentless Huskies Rumble Past Lions

Penn State tried its mightiest to thwart the NCAA championship matchup that nearly everyone was anticipating. The Lions were keeping pace with Connecticut in the second half, both in the tempo of the game and on the

RON CORTES / Inquirer Staff Photographer

Connecticut's Shea Ralph was tightly guarded by Penn
State's Rashana Barnes (right) in the national semifinal.
The Huskies pulled away for an 89-67 win.

scoreboard.

But after about 10 minutes, the Huskies suddenly screamed "Enough!" and pushed the pedal on their speedy transition game to the floor. They ran away from the Lions and gained an 89-67 victory.

The victory assured that the tournament would end on an extremely high note, with UConn and Tennessee, the teams that were ranked 1-2 in the nation for nearly the entire season.

The Huskies, the nation's best shooting team during the season, overcame a cold first half to drain 64 percent of their attempts in the second half. They had to make 10 of their first 15 shots in the period just to keep the Lions at arm's length.

Then the Huskies spurted, tightening the screws on their pressing defense and grabbing the defensive rebounds that enabled them to run. Penn State (30-5), in its first Final Four, simply ran out of gas.

"It was a hard-fought game for 33 minutes, but in the last seven minutes they pulled away," said Penn State coach Rene Portland, whose birthday ended on a sour note. "They did a terrific job on the boards and attacked us in the paint."

The Huskies finished the game with a 42-30 advantage on the boards. Two of their reserve inside players, Asjha Jones and Tamika Williams, combined for 13 rebounds, and Jones also chipped in with 16 points.

The duel at point guard between two of the nation's best, UConn's Sue Bird and Penn State's Helen Darling, went decisively in Bird's favor. Bird sank 5 of 7 three-point attempts and led the Huskies with 19 points and five assists.

Darling, the Big Ten player of the year, endured four

different UConn defenders, including Bird, and went scoreless, going 0 of 6 from the field. She did lead everyone with nine assists and consistently broke through the Huskies' trapping pressure.

Bird, a sophomore who came back after suffering a torn knee ligament just eight games into her freshman year, said the game plan for Darling was to press her because of her 5-foot-7 height.

As for her shooting, Bird said, "I was pretty much open, and it was a matter of knocking it in, and I was able to do that. I was in the so-called zone."

Geno Auriemma didn't spare any superlatives in discussing Bird's performance.

"She hasn't gotten any awards," the coach said. "She's not an all-America, and she didn't make all-conference. But I wouldn't take any other point guard in America ahead of her. That's how good she is. Without her, there's no way that we'd be here. The kid has got a lot of guts."

The Huskies capitalized on their rebounding in the first half to take a 37-28 lead, even though they shot only 38 percent from the field.

The Lions connected on 10 of their first 15 shots in the second half. When Maren Walseth converted a three-point play with 10 minutes, 58 seconds remaining, they were within 57-53 and their fans vigorously shook their blue pom-poms and implored them to overtake the Huskies.

But Penn State cooled off. And UConn kept right on going.

"The last seven minutes, we certainly played at their pace and looked a little tired," Portland said. "They were running right past us and pounding it inside. It got away. Our defense just broke down immensely."

Following Walseth's basket, UConn embarked on a 20-6

Penn State's Maren Walseth went after the ball as UConn's Asjha Jones landed on the floor in the national semifinal.

run over the next seven minutes to take control of the game. Swin Cash, who went scoreless in the first half, scored seven points, including a pair of nice pick-and-roll plays — one off a pass from Svetlana Abrosimova — and a layup.

The Huskies' bench, which held a 32-21 advantage over the Lions for the game, also pitched in. Williams hit a pair of inside baskets, and Kennitra Johnson went the length of the court for a layup. When the smoke cleared, the Huskies

JERRY LODRIGUSS / Inquirer Staff Photographer

A pair of Penn State defenders put the squeeze on
UConn's Svetlana Abrosimova during their semifinal clash.
At left: Maren Walseth.

held a 77-59 lead with 3:55 remaining, a safe-enough margin to have them thinking of Tennessee.

Andrea Garner led the Lions with 19 points, and Lisa Shepherd added 15. But the talk later was of the UConn defense on Darling, who scored 36 points in Penn State's two wins in the NCAA Midwest Regional.

"Our defense at times was lousy. They had more open shots than I'd like," Auriemma said. "But our defense on Helen Darling was good all night. We rotated people and gave her different looks."

Darling said she wasn't frustrated and tried to make up for her offensive drought in other areas.

"It was just an off-night for me," she said. "There's nothing I can do about it. I continued to play hard. I played hard on defense and tried to create turnovers. Offensively, I did not play well, but you have those nights sometimes."

It was one of those nights for Penn State. But it was a good night for the Huskies.

"If you ask anybody who watches women's basketball, their bracket would have UConn and UT meet in the final game," the Huskies' Shea Ralph said. "It's going to be a big battle. But we've prepared and worked hard, and we're ready for it."

— *Joe Juliano*

The key to the victory for UConn, as it had been all season, was that the Huskies were just too physical. Penn State had no answer for that.

UConn's Physical Play Is the Difference

Rene Portland, wearing a fashionable Penn State-colored ensemble, spotted the nuns in Section 115 of the First

CHARLES FOX / Inquirer Staff Photographer

It was a frustrating night for Penn State coach Rene Portland. Her inside players were unable to cope with the legions UConn put on the court.

Union Center a few minutes before the game. They were from her alma mater, Immaculata College, and Portland glowed as she waved to the elderly Immaculate Heart of Mary sisters.

Unfortunately for Portland and her habited fan club, Penn State's game with Connecticut turned more on the physical than the spiritual.

Geno Auriemma went to the Huskies' big bench bodies early, and they were enough to shove the nation's No. 1 team to a victory. Tamika Williams and Asjha Jones, Auriemma's first and foremost substitutes, combined for 26 points and 13 rebounds as the deep Huskies made the most of their height advantage over the Nittany Lions. UConn outrebounded Penn State, 42-30.

As if the opportunity to win a national championship against nemesis Tennessee weren't enough for them, Williams, Jones and Connecticut's other post players played with extra motivation — thanks to Portland.

"Coach showed us an article in December where their coach said they killed us inside in our first game [an 87-74 Connecticut win on Dec. 5]," Jones said. "The thing about it is she was right. We didn't play well that day. So we made sure things were different in this game."

Penn State's big people, Philadelphians Rashana Barnes and Andrea Garner, played gamely but, as the night moved on, wearily. Auriemma's substitution shuttle, constantly shifting Williams, Jones, 6-foot-5 Kelly Schumacher (six points, seven rebounds) and 6-2 Swin Cash (nine points), wore them out inside.

"You know a lot of people ask me if I'm happy here, since I don't start and I come in and out all game," said Jones, who averaged 22 points and 11 rebounds at Piscataway (N.J.) High. "I love it.

JERRY LODRIGUSS / Inquirer Staff Photographer

Connecticut's reserves rejoiced as their Huskies teammates put away Penn State to reach the national championship game.

"You play hard as you can for four or five minutes, going up and down, then you come out and get a breath," she said after going 23 minutes, the same as Williams. "Then you're right back in. It's great. You know Coach isn't going to let you die out there."

Connecticut trailed, 6-5, when Jones and Williams, both 6-2 sophomores, first entered. With Jones collecting eight points and four rebounds and Williams four points and two rebounds, the Huskies built a 37-28 halftime lead.

The sequence that turned this national semifinal around took place with the score tied, 8-8.

Svetlana Abrosimova, who along with fellow all-American Shea Ralph struggled, missed a mid-range jumper, but Jones got the rebound. She turned, lowered a shoulder, and dropped a layup that put Connecticut ahead to stay.

Seventeen seconds later, Williams scored on a layup that made it 12-8. She then stole a pass and fed Sue Bird for a three-pointer. After a Barnes basket, Williams blocked a Garner shot and hit Bird for another three. Connecticut's lead was 18-10 and the tone had been set.

"I felt that if our post players came to play, we'd be OK," Auriemma said. "We didn't get a great game from either Svet or Shea, but that shows you the depth and quality of our team."

Portland knew what was coming. On Thursday, she had said: "They can bring a team of high-school all-Americans off their bench. And it's very difficult to keep up with that."

Even Sister Mary of Lourdes, pausing on the arena's steep steps as, disappointedly, she exited the First Union Center, could see what made the difference for Portland's team.

"We were too dependent on one or two girls," Sister Mary said. "But they had so many."

— Frank Fitzpatrick

Television captured the entire event, with a courtside studio for pregame and postgame analysis.

TV Crew Gives Viewers More Than a Game

Unless you were one of the 20,060 human beings packed into the First Union Center, you didn't see the women's national semifinal games. If you were tuned in, you saw a product packaged and presented by ESPN. That product used the raw material of victories by Tennessee and Connecticut, but it was brighter, more intense, and in sharper focus than the games themselves.

Instead of mere basketball games, ESPN featured well-developed story lines and high drama played out by recognizable characters.

In other words, the women's game was getting the treatment that men's sports have gotten from TV networks for decades. Only the commercial breaks were different, with ads for Monistat replacing the usual beer and tire spots. Nothing tells you who is watching a TV program like the commercials.

ESPN brought the heavy artillery to town for the women's Final Four. The first impression you get looking inside the production trucks is this: They landed men on the moon without this much gear.

From the outside, you wouldn't have believed that the dozens of TV monitors, the high-end computer equipment, the complex control panels, and all the people involved

JERRY LODRIGUSS / Inquirer Staff Photographer

UConn coach Geno Auriemma shared his thoughts on the national semifinals with ESPN's Robin Roberts (left). Penn State's Rene Portland (right) joined the conversation.

could fit into the narrow trailers. But they did, perhaps because none of the space is taken up by oxygen.

The directors, producers and technicians in the trucks worked with the good-humored self-assurance that comes only from routinely doing the impossible under miserable conditions and unyielding pressure, the way emergency-room nurses or air traffic controllers do.

With millions of people watching, Mo Davenport's crews made dozens of decisions a minute. They chose from among dozens of camera shots, different replay angles, and possible on-screen graphics — all the while managing and feeding information to the on-air people.

Davenport is the senior coordinating supervisor for ESPN, meaning that he is in charge of both production facilities. One truck produces the pregame and halftime packages, which are carefully scripted. The other truck handles the game coverage, which is spontaneous and unpredictable.

The people in the truck were nowhere near the basketball court. They saw everything through cameras strategically placed all around the First Union Center.

Davenport was most intrigued by two remote-controlled cameras mounted on the basket supports.

"We're using these for the first time," he said. "They show the game under the rim. Our feeling was that the women's game is defined by the extra pass and the action in the lane. We think this camera will help us tell that story. It might work, and it might not. It's a calculated risk."

It worked beautifully. Some of the most striking images from the semifinal telecasts came from the under-the-rim cameras. The view was from slightly above the action, and the camera was able to smoothly move along with the action.

In the early game, the camera captured a clear picture of Tennessee's April McDivitt taking a knee in the thigh. McDivitt had to leave the game for a long while. In the second game, the camera produced a memorable replay of a Connecticut fastbreak.

ESPN also had cameras mounted on either end of the scorer's table, providing close-ups of the coaches and the players on the bench. In opposite corners were two cameras on long arms that could move them out over the ends of the court.

But those are just gadgets. The trick is to use them in the service of the broadcast. What ESPN brought to town, along with the hardware, was long experience in shaping a major event.

The network identified the main story lines — women's basketball, on the threshold of huge popularity, deciding its championship in a city with ties to many of the coaches and players — and it stayed with them.

During halftime of the first game, ESPN showed the childhood homes of the second game's two coaches. The Broomall house where Penn State's Rene Portland grew up stood in stark contrast to the Norristown rowhouse where Connecticut's Geno Auriemma lived. The coaches appeared live with host Robin Roberts, and Portland talked about trying to hit the driveway basket from her bedroom window.

During halftime of the second game, Tennessee coach Pat Summitt appeared with Roberts. Afterward, an image of Pat's Steaks appeared on screen. The camera shifted to show archrival Geno's. Pat's? Geno's? It was a small moment, but it worked.

ESPN analyst Jay Bilas compared the style of the Rutgers women to that of the Temple men. His comparison held up. Rutgers frustrated Summitt's powerful team with its relentless defense, then faded when it couldn't deliver on the offensive end.

As galling as it is for a print reporter to admit, the story of the game was best told in a quick montage put together in the truck. It showed Tennessee star Tamika Catchings being bounced around in the lane during first-half action, then moving freely with the ball in the decisive second half. Summitt found a way to get Catchings in motion, and that was the game.

In the second game, while Penn State was hanging close to top-ranked Connecticut, play-by-play announcer Mike Patrick and analyst Ann Meyers foreshadowed what would transpire.

The Nittany Lions came out charging in the second half, but Meyers wondered aloud: "How fresh will their legs be by the end of this game?"

By the end, Connecticut had opened a 22-point lead over the exhausted Lions.

To their credit, ESPN's analysts didn't coddle the players. That would be easy to do. After all, the atmosphere around the event was one of reverence for the women's game. There must have been a temptation to treat the players as heroes just for being on the floor. But Patrick and Meyers stressed the disappearance of Catchings in the first half of the Tennessee game and were hard on Penn State's Helen Darling and Andrea Garner. Darling, a star point guard, didn't score a single point, and Meyers contrasted her play with that of UConn's Sue Bird.

And Garner?

"She's going to have to get into this game," Meyers said during the first half. "She's just laying back."

Mostly, though, ESPN's approach was to drop a quick feature about a player into the mix at a strategic moment. It's a trick that works almost like a flashback sequence in a movie, giving the viewer a flash of insight at just the right point in the story.

Tennessee's Kara Lawson had just taken over the game when the screen was filled with an image of her playing football as a little girl. Then came footage of her hero, Mike Singletary, the former Chicago Bears linebacker. That was followed by a live shot of Lawson looking every bit as focused and fierce.

In just a few seconds, by weaving prepared footage into live action, the men and women in the truck were able to show hundreds of thousands of viewers exactly who Lawson was and why her sport deserved respect.

— *Phil Sheridan*

After the first night of games, it was clear to Inquirer columnist Claire Smith that Philadelphia was the perfect location to celebrate the best women's hoops had to offer.

A Superb Site for the Final Four

Philadelphia doesn't often let a national celebration begin without vivid reminders that it is the cradle of liberty. For the national semifinals, this historic town reminded us how very much it remains the cradle of women's basketball.

Two revolutionary wars, not one, began here. The first gave us the Declaration of Independence, the second a declaration that the women's game was big-time and here to stay.

Ghosts of the pioneers from Immaculata, West Chester State, Cheyney State, Penn State and Rutgers long ago gave way to the nation's larger programs.

Present-day powers from Penn State and Rutgers, not to mention mighty Connecticut and Tennessee, showed more than 20,000 of their closest friends that they've handled the legacy well, playing sleek, modern, semifinal games before an enraptured crowd at the most celebrated women's Final Four ever.

As if to prove the first pioneers still very much want to

reclaim the franchise, a determined Rutgers team scrapped for 40 minutes in search of an upset of Tennessee, the team second only to Connecticut in the national rankings.

Rutgers, devoid of an all-American-rich roster but filled with never-ending spirit imbued by its own coaching great, Vivian Stringer, finally succumbed, 64-54, and finished its season at 26-8.

The victory by Tennessee kept alive the Vols' drive to take the championship back to the home it most occupied in the 1990s. Pat Summitt and Tennessee were one victory away from their seventh NCAA crown and fourth in the last five years.

The taut game left Stringer expressing pride in her team's first showing in the Final Four. "We'll be back," Stringer said.

Then addressing the team that always returns, Stringer put it best: "In the breadth of national champions, there's something very special about [Tennessee]."

Standing in the way of Summitt's and Tennessee's ability to reestablish their greatness were Geno Auriemma and UConn, 89-67 winners over Penn State in the other semifinal.

Just like that, the marquee match responsible for the months of intrigue leading to this Final Four was realized, and the nation's top two heavyweight programs got the championship bout most experts predicted.

There were no losers in the Final Four. Not with royalty such as Summitt, and regal record breakers such as Stringer, who coached this area's first Final Four entry in 1982 at Cheyney State. Not with great modern architects such as Auriemma, whose team never slipped from its perch as the nation's top-ranked team.

And not with perennial carriers of the flame such as Rene Portland, who took Penn State to its first Final Four.

All that was needed to solidify the success of this Final Four was the warm embrace of an old friend. Philadelphia delivered.

This Final Four, bolder, bigger, better than anything previously attempted in the women's game, not only raised the roof of the full-to-overflowing First Union Center. The sellout crowd awash in the orange, blue, and scarlet colors of the four schools, raised the visibility of the game so much that the crossover from polite tea-and-crumpets afterthought to a marketable, prime-time event mature enough to dazzle a major-league city was complete.

The descendants of Cathy Rush and her almost mythical Mighty Macs attracted more than 660 media members from all over the nation to this Final Four. Bob Clarke's Flyers didn't do that in 1997 when they were playing in no less than the Stanley Cup finals.

— Claire Smith

VICKI VALERIO / Inquirer Staff Photographer

The national semifinals featuring Rutgers, Tennessee, Penn State and Connecticut drew a sellout crowd of 20,060 to Philadelphia's First Union Center.

Chapter 7

Championship Hype

With the championship pitting No. 1 against No. 2, the hype surrounding the title game was enormous. As big as the U.S. women's soccer team's World Cup title, some said. A landmark event in college basketball, said others. It was Summitt vs. Auriemma, Tennessee vs. Connecticut. What more could hoops fans want?

Heavyweight Matchup: Vols Vs. Huskies

In the city that made women's basketball and cheese-steaks famous, it was only fitting that this NCAA women's tournament came down to a familiar Philadelphia question: Who's better — Pat's or Geno's?

Pat Summitt's Tennessee Volunteers and Geno Auriemma's Connecticut Huskies, the nation's top two programs — in the rankings, in the '90s, in the hearts and minds of fans — would meet not far from Passyunk Avenue, in as tasty a national championship game as anyone could have dreamed of.

"It's kind of like destiny," Tennessee's Kristen Clement

said.

Indeed, this entire season, highlighted by the finalists' home-and-home series, seemed to have been pointed toward a conclusion at the First Union Center.

Tennessee had handed No. 1 Connecticut its only loss. Earlier, Connecticut had beaten Tennessee. Each team won on the road. UConn had won 16 straight, Tennessee 20 in a row. Their rosters were crammed with all-Americans, their schedules with lopsided victories. Their arenas were always crowded.

The nationally televised matchup of two marquee programs was being ballyhooed as a possible transcendent moment for women's basketball, a memorable one that might push the sport to heights long reserved for men only.

Auriemma said it would be like "Houston versus UCLA in the Astrodome [in 1968], but for a national championship."

"I think it's just another one of those events that come along at the right time — the right time, the right teams," Auriemma said. "You're going to look back and say that this was an event that moved the game forward.

"After tomorrow night, the game will be changed. Maybe people will stop comparing it to the men's game and view it on its own merit. We can attract a whole new set of fans who have misconceived ideas about what the women's game is."

Summitt, the sideline-barking advocate of tough love, and Auriemma, the street-sharp coach from Norristown, dominate their sport. This was the 12th Final Four for the Vols' coach, and her defense-oriented teams had won six national titles. The Huskies' coach was in his fourth Final Four, and his team won it all in 1995.

And their battles aren't confined to the court. Auriemma represents the loosening but lingering grip of males on the women's game, while Summitt is the epitome of female success.

The choice for most of the top high school players typically is a simple one: Tennessee or Connecticut.

Connecticut's Paige Sauer and Swin Cash were heavily recruited by Tennessee, while UConn lost Semeka Randall and Clement to the Vols.

The decision by these nonconference opponents to play each other twice was as much about raising the profile of women's basketball as it was about filling their arenas.

"Geno and I talked about this as being good for both programs," Summitt said. "We know it's great for the game. No question that playing them home and home is great for women's basketball. We felt like the best thing that could have happened is to be 1-1. That's what happened. Now we're in the sugar game."

This had become a major sports rivalry. Each team had beaten the other in a previous Final Four; each had won five of the 10 meetings.

"That's what Americans want," Auriemma said. "They love rivalries. Muhammad Ali-Joe Frazier. The Yankees and Dodgers. The Cowboys and 49ers. That was the thinking behind our scheduling them twice this year and next.

"Now, you don't want to overdo it. Half the country loves them now, and the other half loves us. Three more years of this, though, and they might get sick of both of us."

On the court, the story line seemed to be simple. It all depended on how well Tennessee's aggressive defense could contain Connecticut's running game. In their first meeting — a 74-67 UConn win in Knoxville, Tenn. — the

Marci Czel, a senior guard, jumped for joy as the Huskies put away Penn State, 89-67, to earn a rematch with Tennessee in the final.

Vols' defense couldn't do it.

"We're playing the last day, against the last team that's left besides ourselves, and you can't get any better than that," Auriemma said.

And which does he prefer — Pat's or Geno's?

"You been down there recently?" Auriemma said, laughing. "Pat's is old and beat-up and dilapidated. Geno's is bigger."

— *Frank Fitzpatrick*

The Tennessee-UConn rivalry wasn't steeped in tradition, but the 10 previous games had been filled with intrigue, spice and, yes, great basketball.

Tennessee Vs. Connecticut: One Hot Rivalry

The casual fan may still have a lot to learn about women's basketball. But mention Tennessee-Connecticut, and there's a chance that even that fan has an idea that the NCAA title matchup at the First Union Center had the same competitive intensity as a World Series between the New York Yankees and the Atlanta Braves.

"You know the country is always looking for that kind of stuff," Auriemma said. "It makes for great stories, keeps everybody entertained. Makes coaches famous, write books, go on TV, do all kinds of stuff."

The six-year-old rivalry actually began in a subtle way in 1995.

ESPN was looking for a women's matinee attraction on Martin Luther King's Birthday, and it wanted a game between North Carolina, the defending NCAA champion, and Connecticut.

The Tar Heels had beaten the Huskies in a bruising East Regional final the previous season. But they were resistant to playing the game on the road.

Meanwhile, Tennessee and Connecticut had been working on establishing a series, so ESPN decided a meeting between them might be a suitable replacement for Connecticut versus North Carolina.

When the 1994-95 season began, Tennessee, featuring star guard Michelle Marciniak of Allentown, was ranked No. 1 in the nation. Connecticut, featuring Rebecca Lobo, Kara Wolters and Jennifer Rizzotti, was fourth.

But in early December, the Huskies moved up to second, behind the Volunteers. The teams stayed locked into those positions with unbeaten records going into their Jan. 16 game.

An unusually large media contingent for a regular-season women's game crowded into UConn's Gampel Pavilion to see the Huskies put together a solid performance and come away with a 77-66 victory.

The Associated Press held up the balloting in its weekly poll for a day to have the game reflected in the rankings. When those rankings were released several hours after the game, Connecticut was No. 1 for the first time.

UConn continued on its unbeaten road, and two months later, it met the Vols again, this time in Minneapolis for the national title.

In the second half, Lobo led a surge by the Huskies. Late in the game, Rizzotti sped down the court, made a crossover-dribble move on Marciniak, and secured the lead for good for UConn, which successfully concluded a Cinderella season.

In January 1996, most expected Tennessee to get its revenge in Knoxville, where the Vols would be playing on their home court for the first time in the series. They had just set an NCAA record by winning at home for the 69th straight time.

Neither team could gain much of an advantage, but late in the action, Connecticut went on a small run to emerge with a 59-53 victory.

The Vols finally got the upper hand two months later, in the NCAA semifinals in Charlotte, N.C., in what may have been the best game of the series to date.

Momentum swung back and forth, and just when all seemed lost for the Huskies, Nykesha Sales hit a three-pointer to send the game into overtime. But the 6-foot-7 Wolters fouled out for UConn, and Tennessee won, 88-83.

The next day, the Vols gained the national title, defeating Georgia, and Marciniak was name the Final Four's outstanding player.

"When we got to overtime, we just ran out of gas," Auriemma recalled. "And that was as good a game as I've ever been part of.

"I wasn't that disappointed, to be honest with you. I was more disappointed in other games [against Tennessee] that I thought we had squandered our opportunity. I don't think we squandered our opportunity that year."

In January 1997, Connecticut hosted the teams' regular-season meeting, moving it to the 16,000-seat Hartford Civic Center, where it sold out.

Tennessee, which had been hit by graduation losses, had been struggling, even though it had freshman star Chamique Holdsclaw. The Huskies pounced on the Vols at the outset and stormed to an 84-69 victory.

Two months later, UConn lost Shea Ralph, then a freshman, with a knee injury in the first round of the NCAA

RON CORTES / Inquirer Staff Photographer

Kristen Clement accepted congratulations after the Vols ousted Rutgers, 64-54. Clement scored eight points in the victory.

tournament. The Huskies met Tennessee in the Mideast Regional final in Iowa City. The Vols pulled away for a 91-81 victory and went on to win a second straight national title.

In the 1997-98 season, when Tennessee went unbeaten, the teams met just once. The Vols won, 84-69, in Knoxville.

Then some fire was added to the rivalry on Tennessee's postgame radio show. Freshman Semeka Randall, in paying tribute to a crowd that had set an NCAA women's basketball attendance record of 24,597, said she thought the UConn players had been scared. The comment, reported in Connecticut newspapers, elicited a heated reaction from passionate UConn fans.

Connecticut later was hit with more injury misfortune, losing Sales near the end of the regular season to a torn Achilles tendon.

Still, the Huskies advanced to the East Regional title game. But North Carolina State upset the Huskies in that game and moved to its first women's Final Four.

In the 1998-99 season, the teams met in Storrs, again on national television.

Randall, already cast as a villain in Connecticut for her remark the previous year, got tied up with the Huskies' Svetlana Abrosimova while chasing a loose ball. The UConn fans became indignant as Randall tried to wrest the ball free and hit Abrosimova with an elbow. No foul was called. Randall led the Vols to a 92-81 victory.

That set up two regular-season meetings in 2000. Connecticut posted an overpowering 74-67 win in Knoxville in January, with its athleticism a factor. The play of point guard Sue Bird down the stretch as the Huskies doused a Vols rally was a key.

Tennessee evened things up in February with a 72-71

triumph that wasn't secured until the Huskies' Tamika Williams failed to score on a drive inside against the Vols' Michelle Snow.

— *Mel Greenberg*

In the 2000 final, the Vols were concerned about Abrosimova. She learned the game in Russia, then refined it during a love-hate relationship with the equally hard-headed Auriemma at Connecticut.

Abrosimova Has Come a Long Way

One of the first things Svetlana Abrosimova learned when she arrived from Russia for her first year at Connecticut was that Geno Auriemma liked to yell at his freshman players "because freshmen don't know what they're doing on the court."

But when she returned for her sophomore year, and Auriemma kept yelling at her, she thought, "Uh-oh, there's trouble."

The sometimes stormy relationship between the Italian-born Auriemma, one of the most successful coaches in women's college basketball, and the Russian-born Abrosimova, a two-time all-American, is one of the more fascinating subplots in the success story of the Huskies.

Abrosimova is a 6-foot-2 forward who can shoot, rebound and pass. The challenge for her had been adjusting from her status as what Auriemma called "the chosen one" in Russia, where she was MVP in the 1996 European championships, to her situation at UConn, where she was among a group of highly accomplished players.

"He's really tough, especially at the beginning of the year," Abrosimova said before UConn practiced for the final. "This year, he was really tough on me, but I knew what he was trying to accomplish. He proved his point. I improved a lot.

"It took awhile to get used to it. I was working very hard to improve my game, and he saw that. I know why he's hollering at me."

The relationship between this player and her coach received a lot of attention at the women's Final Four, a matter that "everybody is making too much of a big deal out of," Auriemma wearily contended.

"This is no different than the relationship I've had with every one of my really good players," he said. "I don't like any of them, because they are never as good as I think they can be. We're always arguing about how to do things better or differently, and how to improve on certain things. Then after they graduate, I tell everybody that was the best player I ever coached. But while they are playing for me, it's always the same. There's always something that you can pick out that you have to get on them about.

"From where she started when she was a freshman to where she is now, I think she's learned a lot about the game, learned what she can do and what she can't do. She's improved in so many areas as a player, but I think she will be the first to tell you she's not anywhere near where she's going to be four or five years down the road."

Abrosimova first took up the game of basketball in her hometown of St. Petersburg at age 7. Back then, coaches were looking for tall girls to try out for the sport, and she did, although she described herself at the time as "kind of fat and short."

With the help of her mother, who obtained books for her about basketball and encouraged her to improve, she grew gracefully and started to excel at the sport. At 14, she helped her team win the Russian championship. That was when she first thought that it would be possible to attend college in the United States.

Two years later, an AAU coach spotted Abrosimova in a game and notified Auriemma, who dispatched assistant coach Chris Dailey to see her play in the 1997 junior world championship. The recruiting pitch was a painstaking one, because Abrosimova spoke little English and had no idea what a Connecticut was.

"I didn't know about college basketball in the United States," she said. "UConn was the only school to recruit me, but I didn't know if they were a good school or a bad school. I talked to Coach on the phone, and I liked him. He was so nice. He talked to me so loud and so slow on the phone, and that was a good thing for me.

"They sent me a media guide and some pictures, and I was like a little kid. I had never seen anything like that before. So I came here. But I didn't have a choice. No one else recruited me."

The transition from Russia to the United States was a difficult one. Abrosimova missed her family and friends. Although she did well on the Scholastic Assessment Test, she felt uncomfortable speaking English, to the point where "I just put my head down and didn't look in people's eyes."

But her teammates assisted her in adjusting to the new culture and language. Shea Ralph was particularly helpful with getting Abrosimova acclimated, and Ralph benefited from Abrosimova's ability on the court.

"She brings a different style of play to our team," Ralph said. "She's very tough and very brave. She does some things that sometimes Coach doesn't like, but depending on whether the ball goes in or not, that makes up your mind.

"I'd rather be playing with her than against her. She's taught me a lot about the game of basketball, and she's taught me a lot about life."

Abrosimova entered the starting lineup after 13 games of her freshman season and stayed there. The title game marked her 79th consecutive appearance as a starter.

The 1999 Big East player of the year topped the Huskies in rebounding at 6.2 per game, and her 13.4 points were second on the team. Her 14-point, 10-rebound performance in the semifinal win over Penn State marked her eighth double-double of the season and the 18th of her career.

"She's smart, and she's a hardworking kid," Auriemma said. "She has a passion for the game. She thinks the game. I think what she has learned is how to play with other good players, which is going to help her down the road."

— *Joe Juliano*

Meanwhile, Connecticut couldn't overly shadow Tamika Catchings, in fear of allowing Semeka Randall free reign. Were it not for a well-timed telephone call a few years back, Randall could have been playing for — not against — the Huskies.

Tennessee's Randall: A UConn Killer

Semeka Randall strode to the dais, her left hand enveloping a miniature video camera pressed to her eye. As the media horde sat waiting to pepper the Tennessee players with questions about the national title game against Connecticut, Randall panned the room, then, in true form, heckled the audience. She loves to play to a

CHARLES FOX / Inquirer Staff Photographer

Tennessee's Semeka Randall (left) took the ball away from
Rutgers' Tasha Pointer during the semifinal win. At right:
Tamika Catchings.

crowd.

"Oh, this?" she said, looking at the camera. "This is for ESPN, behind the scenes of the Tennessee Lady Vols. You know, the secret stuff, what we do before the game, stuff you want to know about but you can't know about. Sorry."

Then, plugging the forthcoming piece, she added, "Check it out on ESPN."

A national television audience would check her out when she took the court to face the hated Huskies.

Randall's performance would be a key. A 5-foot-10 junior, she was a three-year starter, a Kodak all-American and, dubbed by one writer, "Public Enemy No. 1" to Connecticut fans.

But rewind four years. It was the fall of Randall's senior season at Trinity High School in Cleveland, before she won a share of Parade Magazine's player of the year award. She had narrowed her college choices to two schools — Tennessee and Connecticut — but couldn't make up her mind. Then the telephone rang.

"Semeka," Pat Summitt said, venom oozing from her voice, "you know how badly I want to coach you. Why are you still interested in Connecticut?" Randall just listened as Summitt ripped into her. Four days later, she committed to Tennessee.

Given the heated nature of the Tennessee-Connecticut rivalry, that would be enough to make Huskies fans loathe her. But there's more to the movie, much more.

After scoring 23 points in an 84-69 win over the Huskies as a freshman, Randall was quoted in the Knoxville News-Sentinel as saying Connecticut "about ran off the floor, they were so scared." She insists that her remarks were taken out of context.

Then, fired up for her first trip to Gampel Pavilion the

next season, Randall became entangled with Huskies forward Svetlana Ambrosimova while battling for a loose ball. Randall's physical play drew ire from the partisan crowd, which booed every time she touched the ball. Feeding off the frenzy, she scored 25 points to lead the Volunteers to a 92-81 victory, which ended UConn's 54-game home winning streak.

Randall's take on the tete-a-tete with Ambrosimova: "There were high emotions. She was going for the ball. I wouldn't let it go. She wouldn't let it go. She said I swung her over. I don't think I swung her over, but if she wants to believe that, that's fine with me.

"There might be another jump ball tomorrow when we get tied up again. Hopefully no one will blow it out of proportion."

Ambrosimova said the players had no ill will toward each other, that they even hung out in San Jose, Calif., during the 1999 Final Four. And both players maintain that the event was blown out of proportion. "She's really tough," Ambrosimova said. "She's really competitive."

In 2000, Randall scored 17 points in a losing effort against Connecticut in January, then returned to Gampel to mute the crowd's boos with a buzzer-beating game-winner. Down, 71-70, Randall split two UConn defenders, then double-pumped and popped a 12-foot jumper in the lane over Swin Cash. With 4.4 seconds left it fell through the net, and the Volunteers prevailed, 72-71. Randall finished with 17 points, three rebounds and two clutch baskets in the final minute of the game.

"Semeka gets up for every game, but there's something in the air or something about the name 'UConn' that gets Semeka to step up her game a little bit more," Kristen Clement said. "I think she's going to be very emotional tomorrow, and she's going to try to get the crowd in it."

Added Geno Auriemma: "I love her intensity, and obviously I wanted to recruit her. The energy she brings to the floor and that passion that she plays with is what you want every kid to play like."

Randall spent the summer of 1999 recuperating from surgery to repair torn ligaments in her ankle, then worked on the trajectory of her jumper with a basketball specialist from Pittsburgh because she wanted to be known not only as a defensive specialist, but as an offensive threat as well.

In 36 games, she averaged 14.2 points and 5.2 rebounds. In two games against Connecticut, she averaged 18.5 points and 3.5 rebounds. Her career averages against the Huskies entering the final: 21.3 points, 6.0 rebounds.

Randall wanted to finish filming the Final Four from atop a ladder, cutting down the net. If she was vilified while doing it, so be it.

"I don't feel like I'm public enemy, but if you want to classify me with that label, that's fine," Randall said. "All I do is try to give to my team the best of my ability, and that should take care of the rest. People are going to say what they want to say. I'm not put on this earth for everyone to like. Somebody's got to dislike me in this world, and if it has to be the UConn fans, it has to be somebody."

— *Ashley McGeachy*

With all-Americans on both sides, two of the top coaches in the game and unmatched euphoria, the grand finale was set.

Tennessee, Connecticut Right Where They Belong

The Connecticut and Tennessee women's basketball dynasties, like death and taxes, are among the few certainties left in an uncertain world.

No one with working brain cells really expected otherwise when looking ahead to the women's NCAA Division I championship. The Volunteers and the Huskies were just too good, too committed to their battle for supremacy, to have wound up anywhere but on the floor of the First Union Center for the national title game.

With apologies to Penn State and Rutgers, Tennessee and Connecticut gave the game not only what it wanted, but what it needed for a Final Four show still seeking the broadest appeal possible.

That is not to say the opening acts were not enticing. Penn State and Rutgers gave their all, drawing more than polite applause for their efforts in their semifinal losses. But while the Philadelphia area may have wanted one of its own to reenact a victorious scene from "Rocky II," the rest of the nation was hungrier for much more star appeal.

The nation won out. Those seeking to expand the game by way of national appeal won out. ESPN, a network whose commitment to the game must one day finally be matched by acceptable ratings shares, won out, too, thanks to the most telegenic pairing possible.

"Anyone who follows women's basketball has been waiting for this game," UConn's Shea Ralph said.

The only thing missing was Hollywood premiere searchlights — and a WWF wrestling ring — as the nation's No. 1 and No. 2 teams prepared to put on a grand finale.

"I don't know that it's necessarily a message game," Pat

Summitt said. "I just think it's what a lot of people want to see. It's what [the media] want, the fans want, what TV loves."

Let's face it. No matter the window dressing of politeness or the bountiful respect, these two teams were furiously and constantly trying to elbow each other off the pinnacle. A Tennessee-Connecticut game is often one big flagrant foul, so fiercely is rematch after rematch played.

"We know each other," said Summitt, comfortable with the knowledge that her two-game split with Connecticut proved only one thing: that a rubber match would be needed.

"That's what it's all about; this is what I love," Summitt said. "It's 1 versus 2. Now you get to see some of the greatest players in the game go play at this level with a national championship on the line."

— Claire Smith

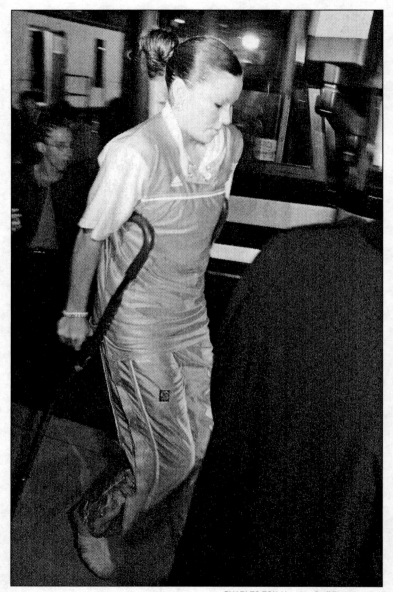

CHARLES FOX / Inquirer Staff Photographer

This wasn't the arrival at the First Union Center that Kristen Clement had envisioned. The Tennessee guard entered on crutches after suffering a sprained right ankle during the morning shoot-around.

Chapter 8

The Philly Final

It was breezy, somewhat chilly outside the First Union Center on April 2. But the weather didn't freeze the pregame spirit of the Tennessee and Connecticut fans. Alas, the Vols fans just arriving for the game could not have known about Kristen Clement's freakish injury incurred during the morning shoot-around, an injury that would sideline her for the biggest game of her career. Before Clement hobbled onto the court for warm-ups, the atmosphere was electric inside and outside the arena.

The Fans Come Out in Force

They'd come dressed head to toe in blue and orange, wearing hats adorned with Husky heads and pom-poms, singing their schools' alma maters and fight songs, yelling "Go Vols!" and "Go Huskies!"

The Tennessee and Connecticut rooters who filled the First Union Center for the NCAA women's basketball championship game — and then overflowed it with their fervent exhortations — were walking-talking-fired-up-to-the-max illustrations of why "fanatics" is the origin of the word "fans."

Supporters of both teams had arrived with sky-high hopes.

"How much better can it get?" exulted Dan Taylor, who in a supreme act of faith and fanatical support for his beloved Volunteers, had driven 10 hours from Tennessee to Philadelphia to see the game, though he didn't have any tickets for himself and his 12-year-old daughter, Katie.

He'd managed to get some — Taylor didn't want to go into details — but "if we didn't get tickets, so what? We'd go back to the motel and watch the game on TV."

Taylor, a 1975 Tennessee graduate, wasn't going to push his luck. Sitting in his car in the parking lot, waiting for the gates to open, Taylor said he had already put in his application for tickets to the next year's Final Four in St. Louis. "We're not going to wait next year and risk missing the opportunity."

Marion Russo, her two daughters, and her friend almost did just that — though it wasn't their fault. Like Taylor, who'd driven up from the South, Russo and her group had piled into their car and driven down from Lebanon, Conn.

Unlike Taylor, they had tickets — they thought. They were supposed to meet a travel agent who'd charged them $250 each for a weekend package. But it turned out the man had taken their money and run.

"We were crying Friday night," said Russo, who was wearing a flashing "Go Huskies" button on her Connecticut sweatshirt.

But "some people with extra tickets for Friday gave them to us, and then people from Rutgers and Penn State

A pair of Huskies fans, Lucinda Belanger (left) and Lynn Bonczek, cheered in the First Union Center's parking lot before the big game.

gave us their tickets for tonight. I tell you, we've met nothing but nice people down here."

Russo's daughter, Joanne Belcourt, piped up from the back seat of their car, "We're having fun again."

There was a lot of that going around. Though the brisk, windy weather was far from ideal for tailgating, many hardy fans were doing just that.

Like battleships towering over a fleet of dinghies, nearly a dozen TV trucks with their satellite dishes thrusting toward the ionosphere dominated the parking-lot scene.

There was little pretense at journalistic objectivity. Several of the trucks for Connecticut stations had "Go

Huskies" posters taped to their sides. Doing their pregame stand-ups, the TV reporters were almost all dressed in either orange or blue.

TV and newspaper photographers roamed through the parking lot, searching for especially photogenic fans.

They literally came at Maite Barainca of West Hartford, Conn., in waves.

Barainca was wearing a blue UConn hat with the fuzzy white head of a Husky on the brim and a blue and white pom-pom streaming out from the back of the hat like the Husky's tail.

She'd waited a whole year for this, having gotten her tickets well in advance. But now that the big game was here, Barainca was very nervous.

"I'm really hopeful that we're going to win, but I'm scared of Tennessee," she said.

"I'm very excited ... but I'm a little tense."

Like everyone else, she was ready for some basketball.

— *Marc Schogol*

Clement was out of the lineup, but even if she had played, she probably would not have changed the out-come of the game. UConn, at least on this night, was too much for Tennessee.

The Champion: UConn? You Bet

His Philadelphia story is complete, with an ending no one, except maybe the coach himself, had anticipated. In the end, he was right: Geno's is better. Geno's is the champ.

In what was billed as a historic national-championship game between the top two teams and the top two programs in women's college basketball, Geno Auriemma's

Connecticut Huskies overwhelmed the Tennessee Volunteers, delivering their slick-haired, street-smart coach his second national title. His first, in 1995, also came on April 2 and also was at Tennessee's expense. But even that win wasn't like this.

That win capped an undefeated season, but it was a close, hard-fought game. This victory was a 71-52 rout played before 20,060 fans at the First Union Center.

When it was over, after the commemorative early editions of the New Haven Register proclaimed UConn "Champs!" and Shea Ralph was named the most outstanding player and the nets were cut down, Auriemma playfully suggested that he was too busy to wait around for a call from the President of the United States.

A White House aide tried to contact President Clinton, who was on Air Force One en route to California. When the aide told the coach he would have to wait a few minutes for the call, Auriemma replied, "I can run out and get a cheesesteak if we don't know what's going to happen. Call me back in 15 minutes, and we'll stay for that long. And I don't mean to be rude, but then we have to have an answer."

Undoubtedly, he would have run to Geno's for a cheesesteak. Two days earlier, he had facetiously declared Geno's better than Pat's, but the proclamation proved true in the title game. With precision, unmatched intensity and a pressing, trapping defense that completely befuddled the Volunteers, UConn embarrassed Pat Summitt's second-ranked team.

The record book proved it. Tennessee's 52 points were the third-lowest total in school history and third-lowest scoring performance in an NCAA title game. The Vols' 16 field goals tied for fewest in a championship game, their 26 turnovers were the most, and their 31.4 shooting percentage was the second-worst team performance of the season. After the first 13 minutes, when the Huskies built a 21-6 lead, the game was virtually decided.

Tennessee never seemed to recover from what happened on the morning of the game. During a walk-through at the First Union Center, Kristen Clement went for a casual, routine layup and came down on teammate Michelle Snow's foot. Clement sprained her right ankle and was unable to play.

The Vols could have used her scrappy defense and veteran leadership. Freshman point guard Kara Lawson lost her poise early and never regained it, missing 10 of 13 shots to finish with six points. Connecticut hounded Tamika Catchings, who got off only six shots but scored 16 points. She was the only Volunteer to score in double figures.

Meanwhile, everything the Huskies did was perfect. Their passes into the post were crisp. Their hands were quick, making 12 steals and blocking 11 shots, including nine by Kelly Schumacher. They shot a solid 44.1 percent from the field in the first half and a spectacular 59.3 percent in the second half to protect the lead they had from the very beginning.

Ralph was outstanding, making 7 of 8 shots to score 15 points. She also had seven assists, six steals, one block and just one turnover. Svetlana Abrosimova added 14 points and Asjha Jones had 12 points off the bench. Both joined Ralph on the all-tournament team, which included Connecticut guard Sue Bird and Catchings.

"This was a great team tonight," Summitt said. "There's no question about it, they were awesome. ... [But] we are not going away. I am not as old as Geno thinks I am,

CHARLES FOX / Inquirer Staff Photographer

Jenna Auriemma (left), the daughter of UConn's coach, and associate head coach Chris Dailey shared a lighter moment during the postgame celebration. A White House operator was trying to arrange a chat between President Clinton and Geno Auriemma.

Christine Rigby (facing camera) celebrated with Sue Bird as

PETER TOBIA / Inquirer Staff Photographer

the realization set in: The Huskies were national champions.

and I'm certainly not on my way out. We'll be back here, hopefully again, next year."

Unprecedented hype surrounded the game. It was billed as a landmark moment in women's athletics, comparable to the World Cup soccer frenzy of 1999. A few days before the final, Bird faked pulling her shirt over her head a la Brandi Chastain, but Bird knew the images of this game would be indelibly etched on the national sports landscape.

It was billed as a landmark moment in women's college basketball. It was No. 1 vs. No. 2, UConn vs. Tennessee. The Huskies had held the top ranking all 19 weeks of this season, the first team to go wire to wire at No. 1 since the Vols in 1997-98. Between the two schools, there were eight high school all-Americans in the starting lineups, the Naismith player of the year, and four Kodak all-Americans.

Moreover, the game was held in the town that for years had been synonymous with women's college basketball — Philadelphia, the town that gave the world Immaculata, Cathy Rush, Marianne Stanley, Theresa Grentz and Dawn Staley.

If there was any doubt, Auriemma had solidified his spot in the Philadelphia hoops annals. In 15 seasons in Storrs, Conn., he had built a powerhouse program, his sideline soliloquies notwithstanding. His 393-95 record gave him the third-best winning percentage among active Division I coaches, and his five consecutive 30-plus winning seasons were a first in basketball history, men's or women's.

He was also king in Storrs again. The scoreboard read: "Auriemma, two titles; Jim Calhoun, one."

"I don't want to share what I anticipated," Auriemma said, "because it will make me look as something other

RON CORTES / Inquirer Staff Photographer

Asjha Jones embraced UConn star Shea Ralph (facing camera) after the Huskies handed Geno Auriemma his second national title. Ralph made 7 of 8 shots in the final, finishing with 15 points.

RON CORTES / Inquirer Staff Photographer

UConn's Tamika Williams went for a steal as Tennessee's Tamika Catchings headed for the floor in the championship game.

RON CORTES / Inquirer Staff Photographer

Geno Auriemma got carried away after his Connecticut players earned the coach a second national title. "It really is an indescribable feeling to win something like this," he said.

CHARLES FOX / Inquirer Staff Photographer

Tennessee's Kara Lawson encountered smothering defense from UConn's Shea Ralph. The Huskies hounded Lawson, holding her to six points on 3-of-13 shooting.

than the way I want to be perceived. I just anticipated a great game, I really did."

— *Ashley McGeachy*

Ralph, the Huskies' emotional leader all season, won the Final Four's highest honor — most outstanding player. She sheepishly accepted the award.

Tenacious Ralph Leads the Title Run

For someone who spent most of the title game scraping the shiny hardwood floor with her knees and belly, Shea Ralph ended it floating on air. Leaping into the midcourt pile of joyful Huskies after their 71-52 win over Tennessee, the Connecticut star's feet looked as light as her heart. And somehow, this hard-eyed junior from Fayetteville, N.C., managed to cry and smile at the same time.

Funny how the horn that ends a national championship victory can turn a demon into an angel.

Stabbing at every pass, stifling Tennessee's best offensive players, making UConn's trapping defense a deadly snare, Ralph was at her snarling, relentless best in a spectacular title-game performance.

She finished with 15 points, seven assists, six steals, one block and only one turnover in being named the Final Four's most outstanding player.

"We just talked about this in the locker room," said Ralph, wearing a championship T-shirt that was as packed with words as her box-score line was with impressive numbers. "There were no MVPs tonight. Everyone did their job. That might have been our best performance of the year, and it wouldn't have been possible if any one of us had fallen down."

Ralph, hearing Auriemma's pregame words in her head, shut down Tennessee's Tamika Catchings for much of the first half and did the same to Vols point guard Kara Lawson. Catchings managed just six shots, while Lawson shot a miserable 3 for 13.

"Coach told me before the game that anytime I saw Tamika or Kara get the ball on the wing, I should leave my man and go trap them. I kept hearing him telling me that. ... It worked really well, and I think that off of those steals we got our offense jump-started right away."

It is difficult to imagine the relentlessly intense Ralph ratcheting up her emotions, but that's what happened. At 8 p.m., more than an hour before the one-sided final began, Ralph sprinted out of a tunnel on the west side of the First Union Center looking as if someone had just sheared off her trademark blonde ponytail.

Her teammates followed. And on this night, even the more typically relaxed Huskies shared her purposeful look.

Center Kelly Schumacher, whose facial emotions generally run from elated to just plain happy, wore a determined grimace and wound up blocking an NCAA-record nine shots. Sue Bird pumped her fist in layup drills and again when she drained a three-pointer that gave UConn a 5-0 lead.

"Shoey played the best game of her life in the biggest game of her life," Auriemma said of his 6-foot-5 center.

But, as usual, it was Ralph who established the emotional tone.

When the referees called the captains to midcourt for pregame instructions, there was Ralph, bouncing on her toes like an eager prizefighter.

"We knew we were going to have to play our 'A' game,"

Ralph said. "We knew we were going to have to be tough and aggressive."

The knockout punch came early. On three straight early Tennessee possessions, Ralph burst through screens for steals. She hit a layup after the first, fed Asjha Jones for a basket on the next, and got the ball to freshman Kennitra Johnson for a third quick bucket that gave the Huskies a 17-6 advantage.

Ralph played furiously in the first half, finishing with seven points, four steals and three assists, but collecting three fouls in the process. She was a like a pinball, bouncing around the interior of the Tennessee offense, trapping ball handlers and forcing Tennessee to tilt. Soon, this ballyhooed matchup was a rout.

"We feed off of our defense," Jones said. "And Shea made that point early. It seemed like she was coming up with a steal every time Tennessee got the ball upcourt."

Jones and her teammates expected that from the all-American who fought back from a pair of knee surgeries and frequently ended practices with bruises, fat lips and bloody knees.

"I don't think there's a worse feeling in the world than playing in a big game and not bringing to the table what your teammates were expecting you to bring," Ralph said. "And then losing the game and having to face your teammates afterward."

She packed a feast.

"Shea is an all-American, so you have to expect that from her in a game like this," Tennessee's Semeka Randall said. "She was everywhere."

Despite her foul trouble, Ralph came out in the second half as aggressively as she had finished the first.

After a fifth steal, she drove the length of the floor for a

CHARLES FOX / Inquirer Staff Photographer

Tennessee's Tamika Catchings landed in a heap in front of coach
Pat Summitt. The 6-foot-1 junior led all scorers with 16 points, but
she managed only six shots against the physical Huskies.

layup that pushed UConn's lead to 34-19. An instant later, she grabbed an offensive rebound, double-pumped, hit a fallaway jumper, and drew a foul.

That caused an eruption among the 20,060 in attendance and a preview of the Connecticut celebration that was to come.

"That was a spectacular play," Auriemma said. "But Shea played a spectacular game."

— *Frank Fitzpatrick*

Equally as spectacular was the Huskies' defense on Catchings, who managed just six shots.

UConn Puts the Squeeze on Catchings

Tamika Catchings was 25 feet away from the basket, right in front of her own bench in fact, as a Tennessee Volunteers teammate tried to throw her the ball. At best, Catchings caught a Connecticut hip.

As the Huskies grabbed the steal and rushed the other way on yet another fastbreak, Catchings found herself under the Vols' bench. She got tangled up with Pat Summitt, who ended up on the floor, too, her own legs taken out on the play.

Catchings was not the national women's college player of the year because she took over a game. She flowed through it. But there was no way through Connecticut. Throughout, the pain of the evening was evident on Catchings' face.

"Come on!" she screamed at a teammate after another easy UConn hoop.

From the start, the night was wrong for Catchings. She picked up the first foul of the game. Her first shot was blocked by UConn center Kelly Schumacher. She lost the ball for a turnover before she took another shot.

She came out and sat next to her coach for a minute, then went in and threw the ball away. She traveled, got fouled, and missed two free throws.

She smiled a lot, looking for foul calls that weren't going to come.

"They came out and just jumped on us," said Catchings, who had 16 points, but just six field-goal attempts, and seven of Tennessee's NCAA championship-game-record 26 turnovers. "They got steals, they tipped the ball, and got hustle plays. They got just about anything they wanted. It surprised me how we came out kind of flat in the first half. Maybe some individuals felt like they had to take over tonight. People were just jacking the ball up."

When she scored her first points on a layup, less than four minutes were left before halftime and Tennessee was trailing by 25-10. She quickly hit another three-pointer but picked up her second foul a minute later and sat down for the rest of the half.

"Everybody was playing individually," Catchings said. "Sometimes we came down, we didn't even have passes. We just shot the ball, and there's no rebounder in there."

In the second half, Catchings tried to lead her teammates back. She hit a couple of three-pointers early. But there was no closing the huge gaps in Tennessee's defense. UConn would bring Tamika Williams off the bench, and she was quicker than Catchings (and everyone else for Tennessee).

At foul-line huddles, Catchings would do the talking, the words flying out of her. But it was doing no good. One time, when Tennessee was down by 17 points early in the second half, Catchings tapped her heart. Her teammates understood the message.

Then Connecticut rebounded its own missed foul shot and put the ball in.

"I kept asking my teammates, 'You guys, we haven't won. Do you guys want to win?' " Catchings said. "They were like, 'Yeah, yeah.' Sometimes it's easier to say something than it is to do it. They definitely came out with more heart than we did — and more attitude and more emotion. Right from the jump. The first basket they made, they were screaming. When we finally made our first big basket, we were like, 'OK.' We just ran back. I was trying to do anything to motivate them. Trying to do reverse psychology, trying to do a little of everything."

At that point, Volunteers sub Shalon Pillow came in for Catchings. But even that wasn't right. Summitt had to scream at Pillow that she was taking out the wrong player. Catchings soldiered on.

"You've got to give credit to Tamika," Kristen Clement said. "Even though she didn't play well, she competed the entire game. There are reasons why she's the best player in the country."

"I have to get stronger," said Catchings, a 6-foot-1 junior. "I think I get pushed around too much, you know. People come at me with the physical mind-set, so I know I've got to work on getting in the weight room and getting stronger."

— *Mike Jensen*

Clement was in agony well before the game started.

For Injured Clement, a Disappointing Night

This was the night Kristen Clement had waited for all season, maybe all her life. This was her chance to play for the national championship in her hometown against archrival Connecticut in front of her family and friends, not to mention millions more on national television.

Suddenly, Clement's dream turned into a nightmare. A collision with a Tennessee teammate during a drill at the morning shoot-around, followed by a piercing scream of pain, changed Clement's status from the starting shooting guard to a spectator at the title game.

The injury was diagnosed as a lateral sprain of the right ankle. In the hours before game time, Clement underwent treatment and suffered through plenty of anxiety while fervently wishing the pain and swelling away.

Alas, all the trainers and doctors in the world couldn't bring Clement around. Arguably the greatest player in the history of Cardinal O'Hara High, she spent the night on the bench, the seat she didn't want to sit in, wearing her earrings and a bracelet with her orange-and-white warm-up suit.

In the end, however, there were no tears. While disappointed that she could only sit helplessly as the Huskies routed her Volunteers, she chalked up her situation to the plan of a higher power.

"It was God's plan," she said in the locker room, the ankle wrapped in ice and elevated on top of a plastic water container. "It wasn't meant to be. He did this for a reason. Sure, it was upsetting, but I've got to accept this and move

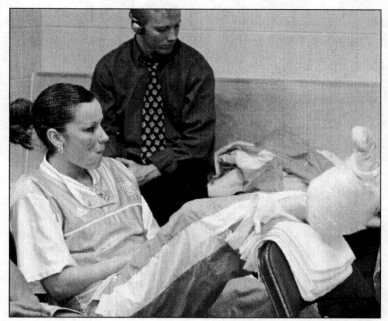

PETER TOBIA / Inquirer Staff Photographer

Kristen Clement rested her sprained ankle after Tennessee's 71-52 loss to Connecticut in the title game.

on."

It had been such a great weekend for Clement. Her outside shooting had kick-started Tennessee early in its 64-54 semifinal victory over Rutgers. She did dozens of interviews and signed hundreds of autographs during her stay in Philadelphia. She even gave her opinion on the city's best cheesesteak. (She chose Jim's, but didn't know the directions.)

Clement's mother and brothers and sisters were in the stands for the final. She was prepared for a duel, mano a mano, with point guard Sue Bird.

Then, the worst happened. Clement rolled her right ankle in the morning collision with Michelle Snow. She spent the day rehabbing the injury. She arrived at the arena on crutches, but suited up and even participated in about five minutes of pregame warm-ups with her teammates, though she was moving stiffly and tentatively.

But her participation in the warm-ups was for support only. She knew about an hour before game time that she wouldn't be able to play.

"It hurt really bad this morning," she said. "I thought if I could rehab it I'd be fine. But when we got to the arena, I couldn't even push off of it about an hour before the game. Before that, I was sort of hoping I could play, but ..."

She didn't finish the sentence. She didn't have to.

Without Clement, the Vols were minus a much-needed ball handler — she led her team in assists — against the relentless defensive pressure of the Huskies. Tennessee finished with 26 turnovers.

Her team also was deprived of a needed presence along the three-point arc. The Vols sank 4 of 7 three-point attempts, but needed more outside punch to recover from the double-digit deficit they stared at almost the entire game. Clement also was missed for her defense.

"She probably is our best defender on the perimeter," Pat Summitt said.

Asked if Clement would have changed the outcome had she played, the coach replied, "I don't think so." But she added: "I've been through this for 26 years, and I've never seen a day like today. You can't lose a player like that and not be affected."

Tamika Catchings said the loss of Clement had a big impact on Tennessee.

"We were ready to play," Catchings said. "Ace brings a lot of energy to our offense and our defense. Our attitude definitely changed without her."

As the UConn lead increased and all hope looked lost,

Clement sat on the bench as dejectedly as her teammates. When the game ended, she patiently waited in line with the rest of the Tennessee players while the Huskies celebrated, and then exchanged handshakes.

"Coach told us we've got to get into the gym a lot this summer," Clement said. "We came back from last year and made it to the Final Four. Next year, we want to be there again and win it all."

— *Joe Juliano*

For much of the night, the focus was on the coaches, Auriemma in his sleek suit and Summitt in hers. Their reactions to the game were as different as their genders.

Style, Strategy, Celebration: It Was Auriemma's Night

The coaching box in front of the University of Connecticut bench was 15 paces long, 1 1/2 paces wide.

It was probably three times the length of the average diving board and about the same width as the common sidewalk.

It was crowded and it was congested with assistant coaches, players and managers.

In the NCAA women's title game, the long, rectangular coaching box was also center stage for Geno Auriemma.

Auriemma, in his 15th season on the Huskies' bench, was part cheerleader, part chess master as the Huskies collected their second national championship.

"It really is an indescribable feeling to win something like this," Auriemma said. "The reason that you can't describe it is you can't put into words the looks on the kids' faces, or what's going through their minds or bodies.

CHARLES FOX / Inquirer Staff Photographer

Geno Auriemma displayed the spoils from the First Union Center basket after his Huskies finished off Tennessee. "I just anticipated a great game," he said afterward. "I really did."

"And really, that's what this is all about. In practice, we tell them every pass, every cut, every rebound, pretend like it's the one that's going to win the national championship. These kids have practiced like that all year long.

"Tonight, when they had to do it, they did it better than any other time this season."

Auriemma, who worked one end of his coaching box to the other, from baseline to midcourt, was up and down all night long, as the Huskies marched relentlessly toward victory.

Auriemma's presence was unmistakable in several areas:

Style. Resplendent in a dark suit, light blue shirt, and matching tie, Auriemma could easily have walked off the pages of a fashion magazine instead of out of the Huskies' locker room.

The jacket came off with 17 minutes, 19 seconds remaining. The tie was loosened seconds later. He returned to his seat while the Huskies warmed up for the second half looking just as relaxed. Connecticut led, 32-19, at intermission.

Smile. Whether he agreed with an official's call (rarely) or disagreed (frequently), Auriemma usually managed to do it with a smile.

Hands outstretched, palms to the sky, he shot that "are-you-kidding-me?" look at referee Dennis DeMayo on one first-half occasion; referee Sally Bell earned the same treatment minutes later. To show he truly played no favorites, he directed the same gesture toward referee Art Bomengen later still.

After one early call went against Connecticut, Auriemma growled: "These guys [Tennessee] are the world's best at taking dives."

Substance. Auriemma is nothing if not passionate. On two first-half occasions, he had to be pulled back from the midcourt area, far beyond the boundaries of his coaching box, by associate head coach Chris Dailey after officials' calls.

Dailey, who towered over Auriemma in her high-heeled shoes, held Auriemma by an elbow as she escorted him back toward a seat he used only on occasion.

When Auriemma bristled at one call in particular, he didn't need Dailey's help. He charged down his walkway and sat himself down. Connecticut led by 13 at the time.

He was equally involved in the second half, even as the Huskies gradually pulled away.

Strategy. With more firepower than any school in the tournament, Connecticut, the nation's No. 1 team, was in an attack mode all evening, both offensively and defensively.

Tennessee lost Kristen Clement, one of its top defenders, to an ankle injury at a morning shoot-around. Huskies guard Sue Bird hoped to capitalize on Clement's absence, pumping up eight first-half shots.

Defensively, the Huskies forced the Volunteers into 13 first-half turnovers, including four by Clement's replacement, Kyra Elzy.

Savvy. With his team leading by 44-24 with 15 minutes to play, the coach was forceful in his instructions to guard Kennitra Johnson. One night earlier, North Carolina had whittled down a similar deficit in its NCAA men's Final Four matchup with Florida, only to fall short in the late minutes. Auriemma pulled Johnson seconds later.

With 9:09 to play and the UConn lead still at 20, 58-38, Auriemma gave an earful to junior forward Svetlana Abrosimova directly in front of the UConn bench.

Abrosimova, hands on hips a foot away, listened silently. She had heard that before.

Celebration. For Auriemma, it began with 1:33 to go when he flashed the No. 1 sign to a sizable contingent of UConn supporters. He shared hugs with Abrosimova and junior guard Shea Ralph when both were removed from the game at that point.

When the victory was complete, he strode to midcourt to exchange handshakes with Summitt. As his players fell on the floor, donning championship hats and T-shirts, Auriemma was swarmed by photographers before disappearing into a sea of blue-and-white humanity. One UConn fan was carrying a handmade sign that said "Geno for Pope."

— Jay Nagle

Try as She Might, Summitt Can't Coax Out a Win

She tried calm.

She tried businesslike.

They didn't work, so Pat Summitt tried angry.

The Tennessee coach was watching the national championship game get away from her talented team. She had to do something. So she turned into Nurse Ratched.

Star Tamika Catchings was the unfortunate soul cast in the Jack Nicholson role from the movie "One Flew Over the Cuckoo's Nest." Summitt stared unblinking into Catchings' eyes and shouted for the duration of a television time-out. Even Summitt's hair looked mad.

Most of what she said was inaudible above the brassy din of the Tennessee pep band, but one phrase erupted at a

PETER TOBIA / Inquirer Staff Photographer

With authority, Pat Summitt made her point during the final. Tennessee's 52 points were the third-lowest scoring performance in an NCAA title game.

decibel level that no trombone or trumpet could hope to outdo.

"Players have to make plays, you got it?" Summitt shouted, disdain dripping from the word "players."

Catchings nodded. Last year, along with Chamique Holdsclaw and Semeka Randall, Catchings was one of "The Mekes." Now, in the face of her coach's fierce words, she was merely meek.

A few minutes later, Catchings scored on successive trips downcourt, breaking her personal scoreless streak and helping the Volunteers to get back into their game against Connecticut. And the next time the team huddled along the bench, Nurse Ratched was gone. Summitt was wearing another face, this time the confident, can-do visage of a big-time CEO.

Summitt seems to decide which face to wear in the early moments of a time-out. She and her assistants huddle first, a few feet from the bench. While they talk, the players are left to their own devices.

This was where Kristen Clement came in.

Always vocal, "Ace" was reduced to the role of extra assistant coach in the final.

While the coaches talked among themselves, Clement leaned over her teammates and shouted encouragement and advice. At first, at least. Like Summitt, Clement changed her approach as it became obvious the Vols were suffering from more than mere early-game jitters.

"We're playing selfish out there," Clement shouted during one first-half time-out. "We're playing selfish on offense and defense. We've got to get the ball inside."

Summitt finished consulting with her assistants, nudged Clement aside and took over the huddle.

During the action, Summitt's face is tough to read. She

sets her lips in a severe straight line and folds her arms. She kneels in front of the bench at times, taking time to talk to specific players or ask one of her assistants for an opinion. It's impossible to tell from Summitt's expression whether the game is going well or badly for her team.

R.B. Summitt was much easier to figure out. The coach's husband sat with their son in the front row of the first section immediately behind the Tennessee bench. A round-faced man with glasses and an orange-and-white striped shirt, R.B. was not subject to the same protocol as his wife.

"Sit down, Auriemma!" R.B. bellowed at the UConn coach more than once. As Auriemma worked the officials, R.B. took exception: "Relax, Geno!"

And R.B. wasn't above letting the officials know his opinion.

"Get in the game, Sally," he shouted to Sally Bell after one physical exchange on the court. "This isn't football, you know."

R.B. Summitt was very quiet in the second half. Almost everyone in orange was quiet in the second half, including the players.

The first sign the game was over came with 12 minutes, 31 seconds left. After Connecticut scored to take a 54-29 lead, there was a TV time-out. The Volunteers jogged to their bench at the far end of the court.

This time, there was no conference among the coaches, no lecture from Clement. The players gathered on the floor in front of the bench. They listened, heads down, as Summitt spoke. This was a new face. Summitt's words weren't audible, but her message was obvious: Finish the season with pride.

When the time-out was over, Summitt handed her message board to a team manager, just as she did after every time-out. This time, for the first time, nothing was written on it.

With about six minutes left and the score an unthinkable 64-39, Summitt walked along her bench and stopped in front of Clement. The coach knelt in front of the player and the two spoke, sharing a quiet moment.

The game was out of reach, but there was still coaching to be done.

Even when it was over. After shaking hands with Auriemma and his staff, Summitt turned and saw her disappointed players walking toward the tunnel to the locker room.

"Hey," Summitt shouted, freezing them in their tracks. "Get back out there and shake their hands."

They did as their coach said.

— Phil Sheridan

The game, although not the nip-and-tuck affair so many observers expected or wanted, culminated a fabulous weekend in Philadelphia, a weekend women's basketball can use to continue to grow.

Women's Game Blooms in Philadelphia Spring

The women's Final Four, which was capped by its biggest gift to the game, a Connecticut-Tennessee championship extravaganza at the packed First Union Center, is marching ever more forward. The weekend lifted the collective consciousness of its increasingly vocal audience of women and girls, lifted it into the mainstream of American sports, and into the view of enlightened sports fans of both sexes. And that is a process that will never be reversed.

Because progress can't be denied, the one-loss-and-out NCAA tournament had no losers, even though only one team walked away with the national championship.

Though it might be hard to convince a thoroughly humiliated Tennessee team after its defeat at the hands of the now-undisputed No. 1 team in the land, there were no losers emerging from this Final Four.

How could there be a loser associated with a tournament that did so much for a game striving so hard to grow?

Philadelphia proved to be a big-league host. The sport proved it deserved the city's effort.

This was a weekend both as tough as UConn desire and as tender as the tears that fell from the players who won it all. The Huskies, avenging their one loss of the season, ended the season with a 17-game winning streak to finish at an impeccable 36-1.

Lest you doubt the Huskies' toughness, consider that Shea Ralph never played a game at any point in the tournament without a limp, a bruise or a Band-Aid.

Yet Ralph was steely enough to score a team-high 15 points, make a game-high six steals, and dish out seven assists in the final. For that, she was named the Final Four MVP.

Tennessee (33-4), strong all season, was hurting on this night — and not only because of the sprained ankle that cost Ace Clement her chance to play a national title game at home.

"We had 26 turnovers," said the Vols' Tamika Catchings, the consensus national player of the year. "They got the hustle plays. They converted on everything."

The surprising rout couldn't stanch the obvious respect among players and coaches any more than it could diminish the vivid rivalry between the teams. There were handshakes and good wishes at the start and at the end of the game, the respect of the competitors for one another not yet ruined by money and as evident in the women's game as the grit.

Most important, the mission still remains clear: Let the girls play.

Every little girl from Philadelphia, New Jersey and Delaware who ever had to legitimize her right to play sports saw a display of powerful endorsements for why her wish should be honored.

Some of the best athletes in the nation were in town, and some were Philadelphians — Tennessee's Clement, Rutgers' Shawnetta Stewart, and Penn State's Andrea Garner and Rashana Barnes.

If ever there was an incentive for this area's public and parochial leagues to keep doing what they are doing — only more — this tournament was it.

This Philadelphia happening was passionate, even compassionate, because it wedded a bountiful number of local stories to the region's historical contributions to the game. So present-day dynasties like Pat Summitt's at Tennessee and Geno Auriemma's at UConn gracefully made room on the stage for Cathy Rush's at Immaculata.

Now the trick is to maintain, not only on a national level, but right here in the shadow of UConn's championship. Area schools can't help but benefit from the afterglow in terms of recruiting and education.

Rutgers and UConn routinely dot Villanova's schedule. So, too, will they grace St. Joseph's along with Tennessee if Hawks coach Stephanie Gaitley's philosophy of building toughness by playing tough teams gets her her desired schedule.

And Temple, too long less than a blip on the radar of the women's game, may be ready to step up to such competition. Ten days after UConn's triumph, Temple named Philadelphia legend Dawn Staley, an Olympian and WNBA star, as its new head coach.

The Philadelphia area launched the modern women's game nearly 30 years ago and hosted its first Final Four, for the pioneering Association of Intercollegiate Athletics for Women nearly 20 years ago.

It now sends women's basketball into the 21st century in good hands. Care for it and nurture it, NCAA, and be sure to bring it back to where it will always be a perfect fit.

— Claire Smith

Chapter 9

===

In the End

*When the fans, teams and journalists had exited the
city to return to reality, it was time to assess the success of the event. By all accounts, PWB 2000 and the
NCAA had achieved their goals — to stage a classy,
entertaining, profitable event that would continue to
elevate women's basketball in the public's perception.
Yes, Connecticut had its trophy and Tennessee had
heartache, but Philadelphia had earned a positive reputation as a host, and women's basketball had
received favorable reviews.*

City's Final Four Effort
Is Richly Rewarded

The organizers of the women's Final Four basked in
praise in the aftermath of an event that was both a critical
and a financial success.

Cathy Andruzzi, executive director of Philadelphia
Women's Basketball 2000, was exhausted but also, she

said, "elated that it turned out as good as we hoped. The fans left here with a great impression of Philadelphia."

"I've been to just about all of them," said Jim Jarrett, the Old Dominion athletic director, who was a member of the first NCAA women's tournament committee in 1982. "They just did a first-class job here. Everything was excellent. The parties were sensational."

The event wound up producing an estimated $25 million in revenue for the city. The games were sellouts at 20,000-plus.

"The Final Four should be here every year," said Doug Bruno, the coach at DePaul University. "It's been great all week. It should be here because this is the place that women's basketball first happened."

Andruzzi said that raising than more than $1.4 million — a record for an organizing committee — "was not easy because of restrictions placed [on us] by the NCAA."

"But the corporate community stepped to the plate," she said. "In the last month, you could really feel the energy that there was going to be a Final Four here.

"Our volunteers did a fabulous job and were prepared. When people stepped off a plane or a train or came across the bridge, they knew Philadelphia was hosting a Final Four."

A Final Four record of 727 media representatives received credentials. The Connecticut team is covered by a large contingent of reporters and broadcasters, and they were on hand for its easy victory over Tennessee in the title game. The presence of Rutgers and Penn State in the Final Four field attracted large numbers of reporters from New Jersey and from across Pennsylvania.

Fans at the sold-out First Union Center consumed 568 pounds of hot dogs, 264,580 ounces of popcorn, 5,955 soft pretzels, 3,173 gallons of soda, 2,564 personal-size pizzas, 840 pounds of steak, 389 gallons of ice cream, and 2,769 pounds of french fries, according to arena officials.

— *Mel Greenberg*

Auriemma, for one, had positive vibes about the event's success story.

A Big Step for the Women's Game

Geno Auriemma thought the sport had benefited from having the Final Four in a Northeastern city.

"The media have embraced it," the UConn coach said. "The city has embraced it. It's not in a small community where people could say, 'Well, it's an isolated incident where they like women's basketball.'

"This is Philadelphia. And Philadelphia is a pro sports town. And at the same time, they've taken women's basketball and really elevated the coverage of it and the enthusiasm of it."

The scope of the attention surprised Cecelia Carter-Smith, a writer from the Hamilton Spectator in Ontario.

"I'm just flabbergasted and overwhelmed," she said. "It's just incredible. I haven't been able to sleep, I'm so excited.

"The downside in our country is, this is on ESPN, and no one gets that," Carter-Smith said. "I just came from our men's finals, and it can't compare to this. It was inside a venue-arena that seats 10,000 people and it didn't even sell out. And it had the top two teams in the country. It should be like this all the time."

Jeff Metcalfe, who has covered women's collegiate and professional basketball for the Arizona Republic, tempered the notion that the final was a watershed event in the sport's growth.

"It's like apples and oranges," Metcalfe said. "Since 1995, when Connecticut and Tennessee played for the NCAA title, there have been many moments in women's sports. You had the 1996 Olympics and the way U.S. women excelled. Then came pro basketball, and we've had three summers in the WNBA. Last summer there were the big crowds and attention over the U.S. women's soccer team and the World Cup."

Chuck Schoffner, the Associated Press' national women's basketball reporter, said the Final Four teams and the First Union Center were a good mix.

"First, the arena was wonderful and gives it a big-time look," Schoffner said. "Then, the crowd was wonderful Friday night and really into the game. Although a lot of people decry the lack of upsets and parity in the tournament, I think in this sport, it's still helpful for the best teams to move forward at this point in time."

Barbara Jacobs, the supervisor of officials in the Big East Conference and former Syracuse coach, had attended the women's Final Four since its inception in 1982.

"A lot of times people thought this could not happen in a major city in the Northeast," Jacobs said. "People wouldn't come out and see the games. But the media attention it has drawn says, 'Hey, this can be done. And it can have a lot of fan support.'

"We used to go to places where the game was popular in the hometowns of teams such as Tennessee. Now it's, 'Hey, we don't have to do that anymore.' "

Still, there are challenges ahead. After the 2001 Final Four in St. Louis, the event will spend three years in domed arenas — in 2002, the Alamodome in San Antonio,

Texas; in 2003, the Georgia Dome in Atlanta; and in 2004, the Louisiana Superdome in New Orleans.

And when the new TV contract is negotiated for the 2002 season, attempts will be made to schedule the Final Four and regional games differently to avoid being overshadowed by the men's tournament games.

— *Mel Greenberg*

Thoughts turned to the future and returning the Final Four to the Northeast, if not Philadelphia.

Why Not a Garden Party for the Final Four?

The leaders of Philadelphia Women's Basketball 2000 were told repeatedly how this city raised the bar for future Division I basketball championships.

The organizers deserved the applause. The city deserved the credit. Now let's see if the women's wing of the NCAA sees the light. If ever there was a display of what a region can do for a sport, it was found here, at the first Final Four played in a major East Coast city.

We know the women's Final Four won't come this way again soon. Such events are planned far into the future, and the next four women's finals will play out in different regions and time zones — and move into domed stadiums.

Thinking big shouldn't prevent the NCAA from getting back to the game's roots at the earliest opportunity.

Think New York and Madison Square Garden, NCAA. Think Boston and that second-generation parquet floor. Most of all, think Philadelphia, again, because Philadelphia is surely thinking NCAA.

"The Northeast is where we need to be," Cathy

Andruzzi said. "It's critical for the game to stage major women's sporting events, and I'd like to see Philadelphia very much be a part of continuing that momentum."

It is now a proven fact that the women's game can benefit from pursuing cities that embrace the city game.

So enjoy those interchangeable behemoth domes before they all go the way of the dinosaur or the Astrodome (abandoned) or the Kingdome (kaboom!). Then think Philadelphia.

Andruzzi and her committee already started thinking 2005 — the next available Final Four date — before the signage came down at the First Union Center. PWB 2000 sees no reason to go out of business. Instead, the most ambitious promoter of women's sports in the city will continue stoking the engine in an effort to keep the city in the lead.

"The next step is bringing a regional here," said Andruzzi. "Then we look to the next available Final Four."

Philadelphia organizers earned the right to flex their muscles by producing an event that generated an estimated $25 million in revenue for the city. The NCAA can't as easily measure what the increased exposure means for it. Why shouldn't the NCAA eye other East Coast basketball bastions usually reserved for the men's game?

It can no longer be assumed that New York and Boston would be indifferent to hosting the women, not after seeing the crowds of more than 20,000 at the First Union Center.

"At our farewell luncheon, Bernadette McGlade, the chairman of the women's basketball committee, said it best when she said Philadelphia had just staged the best Final Four, ever," Andruzzi said.

Just the knowledge that the First Union Center sold out months before anyone knew that the Final Four would consist of UConn, Tennessee, Rutgers and Penn State altered perceptions that women's games were not big enough for big-league cities in the East.

The Baltimore-Washington area proved its acceptance of the women's game by supporting the wildly popular WNBA Mystics. New York showed its intentions when it hosted a celebrity-studded WNBA all-star extravaganza at the Garden just months after more than 15,000 fans filled the same building to see Tennessee play Rutgers.

Imagine what the attendance might be if those same two teams appeared in a Final Four game in the Big Apple. Or, more intriguing, consider a Garden tilt between UConn — the pride of the Big East — and emerging power Rutgers, the self-declared Jewel of the East.

New York would know what to do with such delicious possibilities. Philadelphia certainly did.

— Claire Smith

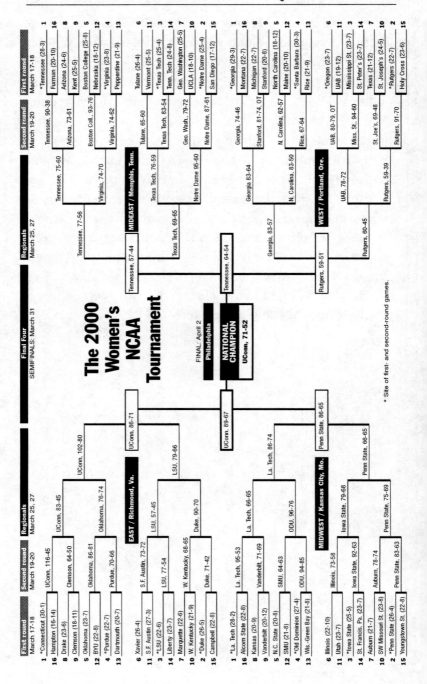

The 2000 Women's NCAA Tournament

NATIONAL CHAMPION
UConn, 71-52

FINAL: April 2
Philadelphia

Final Four
SEMIFINALS: March 31

EAST / Richmond, Va.

MIDEAST / Memphis, Tenn.

MIDWEST / Kansas City, Mo.

WEST / Portland, Ore.

* Site of first- and second-round games.

First round — March 17-18

1 *Connecticut (30-1)
16 Hampton (16-14)
8 Drake (23-6)
9 Clemson (18-11)
5 Oklahoma (23-7)
12 BYU (22-8)
4 *Purdue (22-7)
13 Dartmouth (20-7)
6 Xavier (26-4)
11 S.F. Austin (27-3)
3 *LSU (22-6)
14 Liberty (23-7)
7 Marquette (22-6)
10 W. Kentucky (21-9)
2 *Duke (26-5)
15 Campbell (22-8)

1 *La. Tech (28-2)
16 Alcorn State (22-8)
8 Kansas (20-9)
9 Vanderbilt (20-12)
5 N.C. State (20-8)
12 SMU (21-8)
4 *Old Dominion (27-4)
13 Wis.-Green Bay (21-8)
6 Illinois (22-10)
11 Utah (23-7)
3 *Iowa State (25-5)
14 St. Francis, Pa. (23-7)
7 Auburn (21-7)
10 SW Missouri St. (23-8)
2 *Penn State (26-4)
15 Youngstown St. (22-8)

1 *Tennessee (28-3)
16 Furman (20-10)
8 Arizona (24-6)
9 Kent (25-5)
5 Boston College (25-8)
12 Nebraska (18-12)
4 *Virginia (23-8)
13 Pepperdine (21-9)
6 Tulane (26-4)
11 Vermont (25-5)
3 *Texas Tech (25-4)
14 Tenn. Tech (24-8)
10 Geo. Washington (25-5)
7 UCLA (18-10)
2 *Notre Dame (25-4)
15 San Diego (17-12)

1 *Georgia (29-3)
16 Montana (22-7)
8 Michigan (22-7)
9 Stanford (20-8)
5 North Carolina (18-12)
12 Maine (20-10)
4 *Santa Barbara (30-3)
13 Rice (21-9)
6 *Oregon (23-7)
11 UAB (19-12)
3 Mississippi St. (23-7)
14 St. Peter's (23-7)
7 Texas (21-12)
10 St. Joseph's (24-5)
2 *Rutgers (22-7)
15 Holy Cross (23-6)

Second round — March 19-20

UConn, 116-45
Clemson, 64-50
Oklahoma, 86-81
Purdue, 70-66
S.F. Austin, 73-72
LSU, 77-54
W. Kentucky, 68-65
Duke, 71-42

La. Tech, 95-53
Vanderbilt, 71-69
SMU, 64-63
ODU, 94-85
Illinois, 73-58
Iowa State, 92-63
Auburn, 78-74
Penn State, 83-63

Tennessee, 90-38
Arizona, 73-61
Boston Coll., 93-76
Virginia, 74-62
Tulane, 65-60
Texas Tech, 83-54
Geo. Wash., 79-72
Notre Dame, 87-61

Georgia, 74-46
Stanford, 81-74, OT
N. Carolina, 62-57
Rice, 67-64
UAB, 80-79, OT
Miss. St., 94-60
St. Joe's, 69-48
Rutgers, 91-70

Regionals — March 25, 27

UConn, 83-45
Oklahoma, 76-74
LSU, 57-45
Duke, 90-70

La. Tech, 66-65
ODU, 96-76
Iowa State, 79-68
Penn State, 75-69

Tennessee, 75-60
Virginia, 74-70
Texas Tech, 76-59
Notre Dame 95-60

Georgia, 83-64
N. Carolina, 83-50
UAB, 78-72
Rutgers, 60-45

UConn, 102-80
LSU, 79-66
La. Tech, 86-74
Penn State, 66-65

Tennessee, 77-56
Texas Tech, 69-65
Georgia, 83-57
Rutgers, 59-51

UConn, 86-71
La. Tech, 86-71

Tennessee, 57-44
Rutgers, 59-51

UConn, 89-67
Tennessee, 64-54

Acknowledgements

Many people worked many days, nights, weekends and holidays to write, edit and produce the body of work contained in this book.

I would like to thank the immensely talented Inquirer writers who produced wonderful stories under the pressure of maddening deadlines.

There were other people behind the scenes who worked just as hard, but without getting the public recognition that goes along with a byline.

Sandra Long was instrumental in the planning of this book, of all the Final Four coverage, and in putting together the space needed to present the work in an attractive package. Karen Knoll took the idea of creating a book and quickly made it real. Thanks to Dick Cooper for showing us the way.

I'd like to thank Rob King, The Inquirer's deputy sports editor, for his energy, vision and creativity. Mike Leary, Bruce Martin, Gary Miles, Robin Smith, Chuck Newman and Lou Rabito helped to drive the coverage of women's basketball all season long and in the frenzy of the Final Four.

The news desk, particularly Reid Tuvim, Brent Larson, Steve Kelly, Charles Knittle and Chris Vivlamore, pulled everything together and created beauty out of chaos. Oscar Miller and the sports copy desk fine-tuned the articles.

Photo editors Clem Murray, Mari Schaefer, Ed Hille and Jay Talbot culled the best work of The Inquirer's wonderful photographers, including Vicki Valerio, who spent more time at women's basketball games this season than Mr. Basketball himself, Mel Greenberg. Well, almost more time than Mel.

Staff artist John Duchneskie produced some MVP artwork during the Final Four. Matthew Ericson designed this book with his usual aplomb. Also, thanks to Dylan Purcell for his computer wizardry and Olga McVey and Kara Parfitt for their support.

The staff of Philadelphia Women's Basketball 2000 was helpful all season long, as were the administrations of the two host schools, the University of Pennsylvania and St. Joseph's University. I would particularly like to thank the coaching staff and administration at St. Joe's: Stephanie Gaitley, Frank Gaitley, Nikki Jones, Reggi Grennan, Larry Dougherty and Phil Denne.

Finally, I would like to thank Jim Swan's children, Jessica, Jimmy and Tracy, for allowing their dad to spend countless hours pulling all the material together and editing the book.

Timothy Dwyer
Inquirer Sports Editor